LOST
CANOE
ROUTES

ONTARIO'S
LOST
CANOE
ROUTES

Kevin Callan

The BOSTON
MILLS PRESS

National Library of Canada Cataloging in Publication Data

Callan, Kevin
    Ontario's lost canoe routes

Includes bibliographical references.
ISBN 1-55046-388-8

1. Canoes and canoeing – Ontario – Guidebooks. 2. Ontario – Guidebooks. I. Title.

GV776.15.O5C3446 2002
797.1'22'09713   2002-900603-1

Copyright © 2002 Kevin Callan

05 04 03 02 01   1 2 3 4 5

Published in 2002 by
Boston Mills Press
132 Main Street
Erin, Ontario N0B 1T0
Tel 519-833-2407
Fax 519-833-2195
e-mail books@bostonmillspress.com
www.bostonmillspress.com

An affiliate of
Stoddart Publishing Co. Limited

895 Don Mills Road
#400 2 Park Centre
Toronto, Ontario
Canada M3C 1W3
Tel 416-445-3333
Fax 416-445-5967
e-mail gdsinc@genpub.com

Distributed in Canada by
General Distribution Services Limited
325 Humber College Boulevard
Toronto, Canada M9W 7C3
Orders 1-800-387-0141 Ontario & Quebec
Orders 1-800-387-0172 NW Ontario
    & other provinces
e-mail customer.service@genpub.com

Distributed in the United States by
General Distribution Services Inc.
PMB 128, 4500 Witmer Industrial Estates
Niagara Falls, New York 14305-1386
Toll-free 1-800-805-1083
Toll-free fax 1-800-481-6207
e-mail gdsinc@genpub.com
www.genpub.com

Cover design by Gillian Stead
Interior design by Mary Firth
Photos by Kevin Callan
Maps by Tim Wykes
Printed in Canada

We acknowledge for their financial support of our publishing program the Canada Council, the Ontario Arts Council, and the Government of Canada through the Book Publishing Industry Development Program (BPIDP).

CONTENTS

Acknowledgments 7

Preface 8

1. Wabakimi Provincial Park 10
2. Steel River Loop 22
3. Chapleau and Nemegosenda Rivers 36
4. Wakami Lake Loop 54
5. Ranger Lake Loop 62
6. Dunlop Lake Loop 74
7. Lac aux Sables: Bark Lake Loop 84
8. Nabakwasi River Loop 94
9. Four M Circle Loop 102
10. Tatachikapika River 110
11. Chiniguchi River 120
12. Temagami's Canton Lakes 128
13. Marten River Provincial Park 138
14. South River 144
15. York River 156

Bibliography 164

6   ONTARIO'S LOST CANOE ROUTES

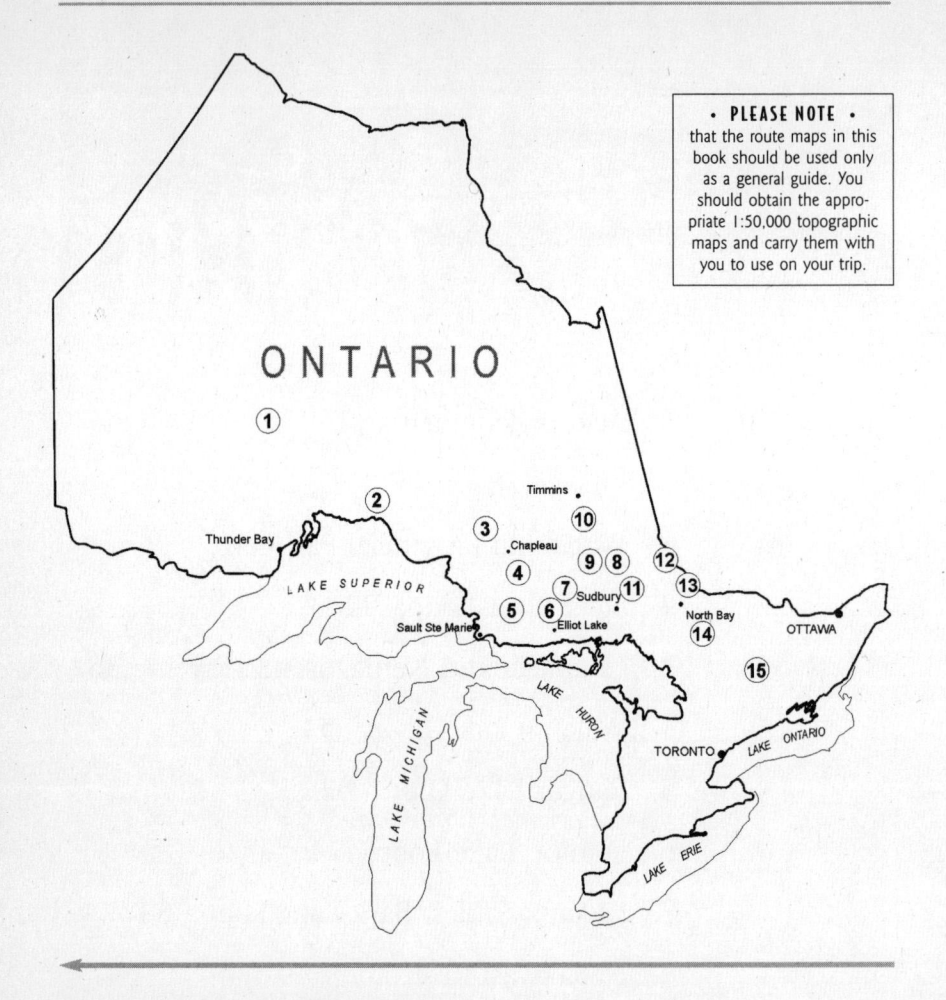

> **• PLEASE NOTE •**
> that the route maps in this book should be used only as a general guide. You should obtain the appropriate 1:50,000 topographic maps and carry them with you to use on your trip.

RAPID CLASSIFICATION SYSTEM

- **CLASS I**   Easy to moderate whitewater with an obvious route choice.
- **CLASS II** Moderate to difficult whitewater but still has a recognizable and clear passage through.
- **CLASS III** Difficult whitewater that requires initial scouting and advanced paddling skills. Experience is essential.
- **CLASS IV** Extremely difficult whitewater that requires precise maneuvering. Should not be attempted while on a wilderness trip.
- **CLASS V**   Suicidal!
- **CBR**   "Check Before Running" indicates that the rapid is more difficult than it initially seems.

SOMETHING TO THINK ABOUT...

"I always think rating rapids is sort of a silly thing, because if you tip over in a one, that's a five to you."
                                                        Robert Perkins, *Talking to Angels*

ACKNOWLEDGMENTS

I THINK THIS HAS BEEN PERHAPS my most difficult, yet worthwhile book. And it wouldn't have been possible to complete without the help of many generous people. I would first like to thank my canoe companions who agreed to "get lost" with me: Scott Roberts; Kevin Foley; Peter Fraser; Mike Walker; Doug Galloway; Scott Bowers; Andy Baxter; Kip Spidell; Nancy Scott; Bob Knudsen; Hugh Banks; Boris Swidersky; Fred Shuttleworth; Jaime Sculthorpe; Matt McPhersey; Teresa Clayton; Dave and Julie Preslie (and dog Louie); the gang at Gulliver's book store (Suzanne and Bernie Brooks, Carrie and Jean Audette, and dog Charlie); Noel Hudson; my dog, Bailey; and especially my wife, Alana.

Thanks also goes out to Tim Wykes for creating exceptional maps for the book; editor Kathy Fraser and designer Mary Firth for their outstanding talents; the staff at *Explore* magazine, Wildrock Outfitters, and Trent Photographics for all their assistance and enthusiasm throughout the years; Jim Stevens at Eureka Packs and Tents; Bill at Ostrom Packs; Glenn Fallace from Voyageur Canoe; and all the gang at Dagger for supplying me with some great gear on this and other writing projects.

A special note of gratitude goes out to Mountain Equipment Co-op for agreeing to help maintain a number of the canoe routes recorded in this guide by way of their Social and Environmental Responsibility Program. With the dedication of organizations like Mountain Equipment Co-op, Ontario's lost canoe routes may soon be "rediscovered."

Finally, I would like to thank the wilderness I have traveled through. It has added immeasurably to my life.

PREFACE

IN THE SPRING OF 2000, I had a nasty run-in with some extremely unethical canoeists on an overcrowded portage. After that experience, I began looking for "lost" canoe routes across Ontario. It became a personal quest, looking for a way to escape the business of the province's well-known parks. Places like Algonquin and Killarney are great, but everybody knows about them. It took some time to get used to the challenges of bushwhacking through grown-over portages and being continuously confused as to my whereabouts. The word "lost" was particularly appropriate many times. But the rewards were high. I never once had to reserve a campsite, and hardly ever had to deal with anything even resembling a crowd. And few unscrupulous canoeists choose to travel these routes, so run-ins were rare.

Two years later — in all, ninety-four days spent in a canoe — I had become obsessed with the unfamiliar. I had fallen addicted to these obscure routes and, at the same time, became totally dedicated to the protection of them.

Hmmm, you may be thinking. How can a route be "lost," or better yet, protected, if some wilderness pornographer like me writes about it in a guidebook? Well, in this day and age, it seems the only way to actually save something is to make use of it. I admit to having a bit of a problem with this philosophy. After all, true wilderness is a place we've never been. But I also don't want Ontario's prime canoe routes to disappear entirely. So they must be publicized if they are to survive. I do believe this.

One of the big questions we should be asking ourselves is why are these canoe routes lost in the first place?

First of all, the government, while creating dozens of new provincial parks through the Living Legacy program, has also severely cut back on ways for canoeists to visit them. To date, not one newly created park has a properly managed canoe route. And a large number of canoe routes in previously protected areas are also not being maintained.

Second, canoe tripping itself has dramatically changed over the past couple of decades. Guidebooks written twenty years ago had trips ranging from eight to ten days. Now they average three to five days at most. The distance canoe trippers once traveled to reach wilderness areas was at least a day's drive. Now it's less than two hours. Even the difficulty of the route has altered. Paddlers are now equipped with lighter boats and much more advanced gear, but the idea of portaging over a kilometer seems insane to most.

This shift in ideas is not necessarily a bad thing. It's a constantly changing society. People are busier at work. Our time is limited. And when you do go on a stress-relief holiday, you don't necessarily want to spend most of that time balancing a canoe over your head.

Believe me, though — these lost canoe routes are well worth the time and effort, both for the government to manage them and for canoeists to travel on them. The inspiring scenery along the Steel River, the continuous swift water of Tatachikapika River, the old-growth pine of Algoma's Ranger Lake Loop, Wabakimi's elusive woodland caribou and the bizarre hermitage of Wendell Beckwith — all are worth being rediscovered and, it is hoped, cherished forever.

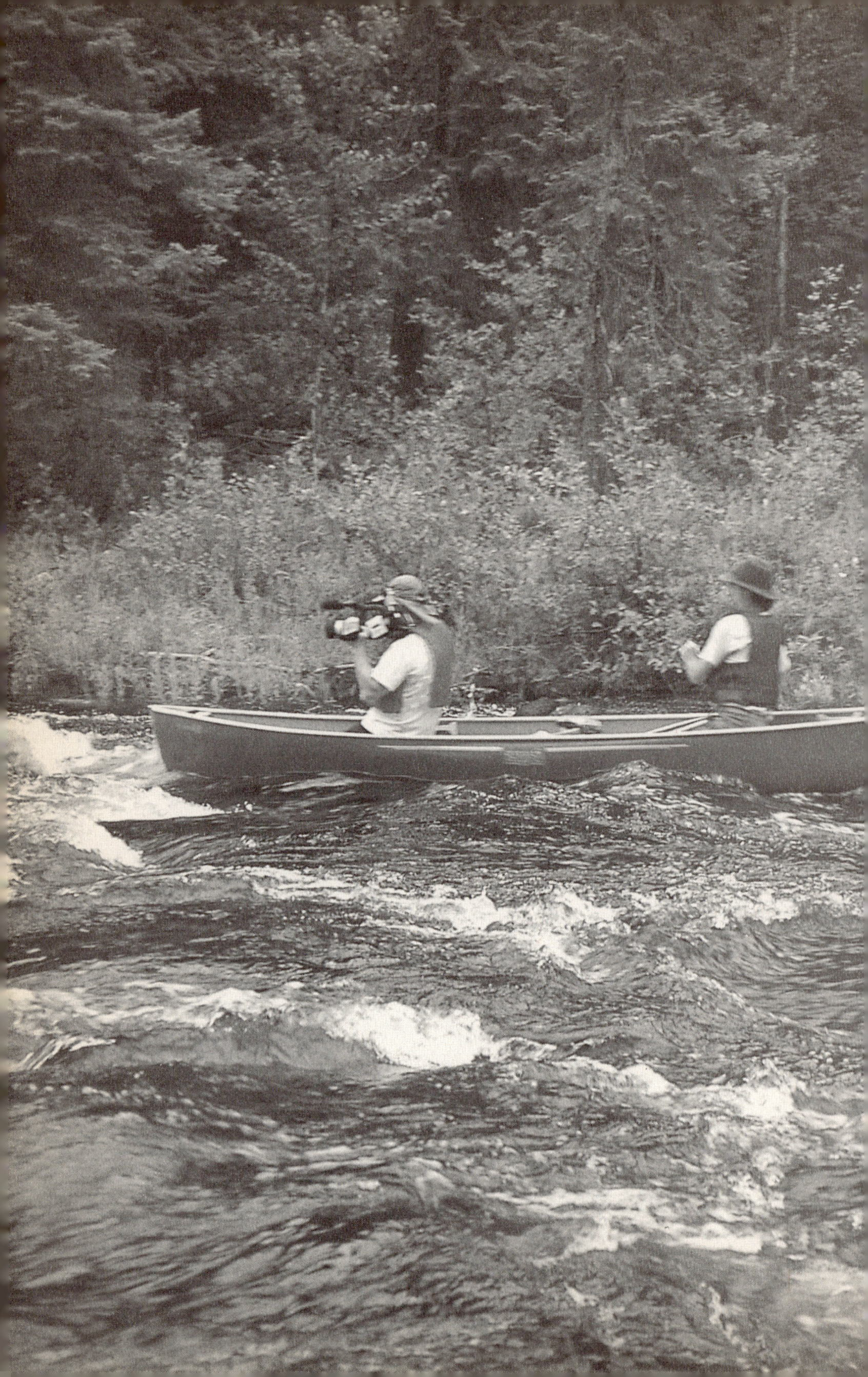

WABAKIMI
PROVINCIAL PARK

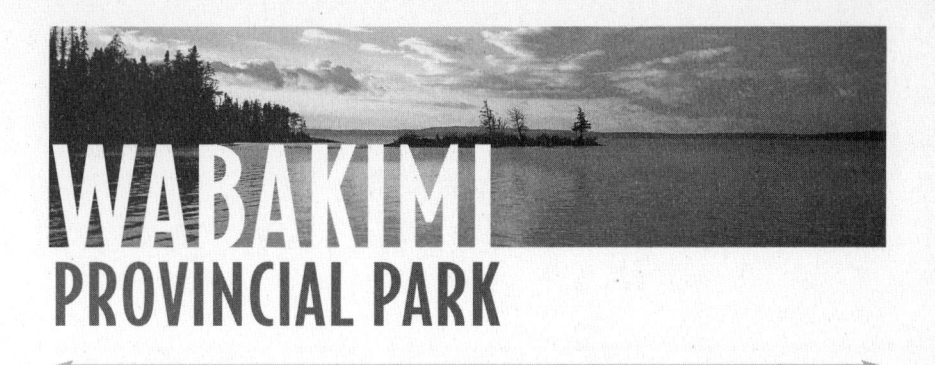

IT WAS NANCY SCOTT, A PARK PLANNER for Ontario, who first got me intrigued with the idea of paddling in Wabakimi Provincial Park, located 300 kilometers north of Thunder Bay. The fact that the park measures almost one million hectares in size and contains over 2,000 kilometers of canoe trails was enough to catch my interest. But it was Nancy's story of eccentric inventor Wendell Beckwith, who lived alone for twenty years on Wabakimi's Whitewater Lake to devote his life to "pure" research, that finally convinced me to give this massive chunk of solitude a try.

Joining me on the pilgrimage to the Beckwith site was film producer Kip Spidell. It was our first trip together, but he was convinced that if he followed a bumbling canoehead like me through the wilderness for eight days, he'd get enough good film footage to make the trip worth his while.

Mercifully, Nancy also agreed to tag along as guide. Not only did she know the exact whereabouts of Wendell's hermitage on Whitewater Lake, but she also knew the locations of all the unmarked portages and campsites along the way — a bonus for any group traveling in such a remote park, where woodland caribou far outnumber the canoeists.

The three possible ways to access the park are road, rail and floatplane. The road is obviously the cheapest, but not necessarily the best overall. It's a relatively easy drive to the launch on Caribou Lake, 12 kilometers north of Armstrong via the Armstrong Road (Highway 527) and then Caribou Lake Road. But the full day's paddle across the expanse of Caribou Lake to the actual park boundary can be a real bore, not to mention extremely hazardous should the wind pick up.

Kip and I filming the wilds of Wabakimi (Lookout River). PHOTO: NANCY SCOTT

12 ONTARIO'S LOST CANOE ROUTES

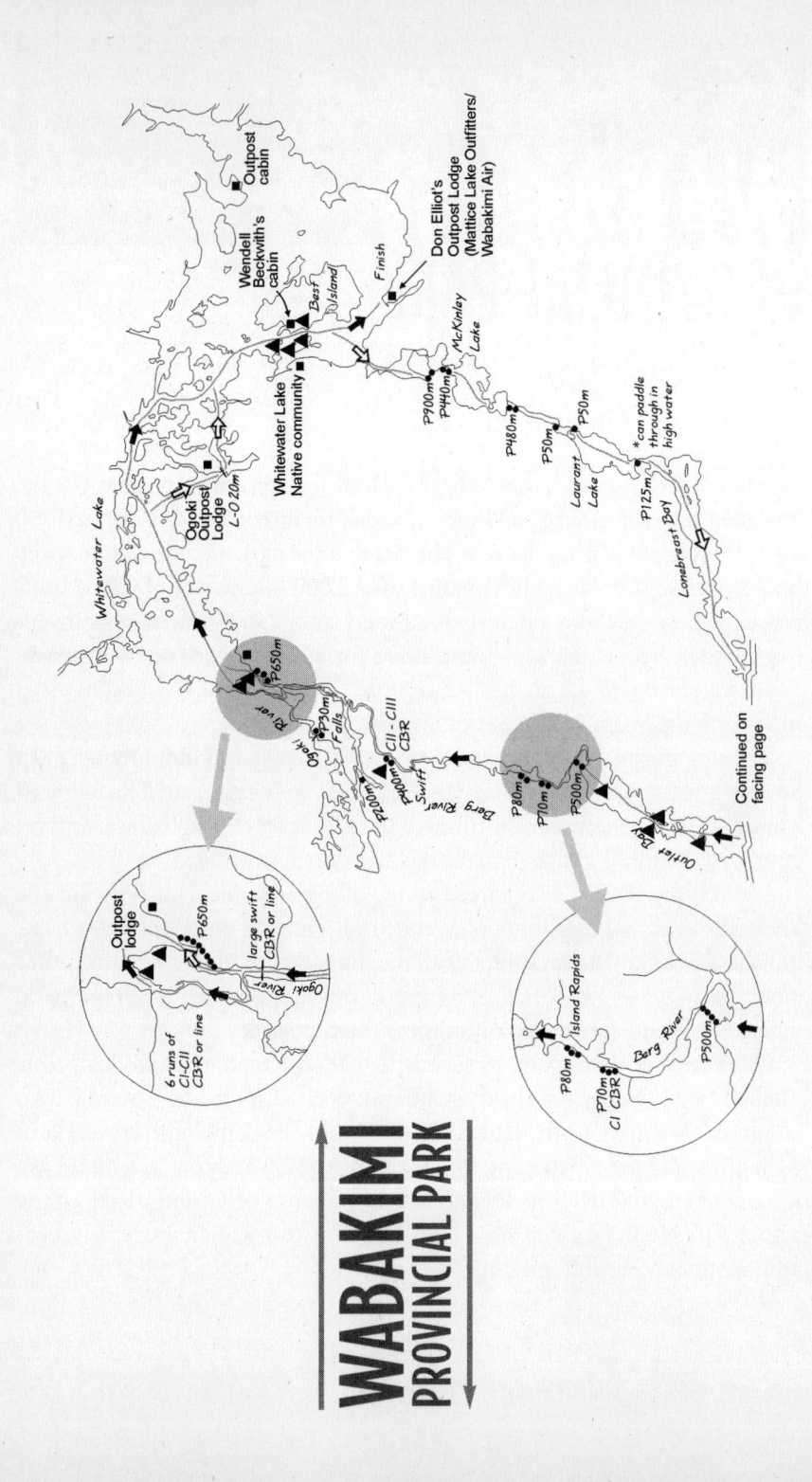

WABAKIMI PROVINCIAL PARK 13

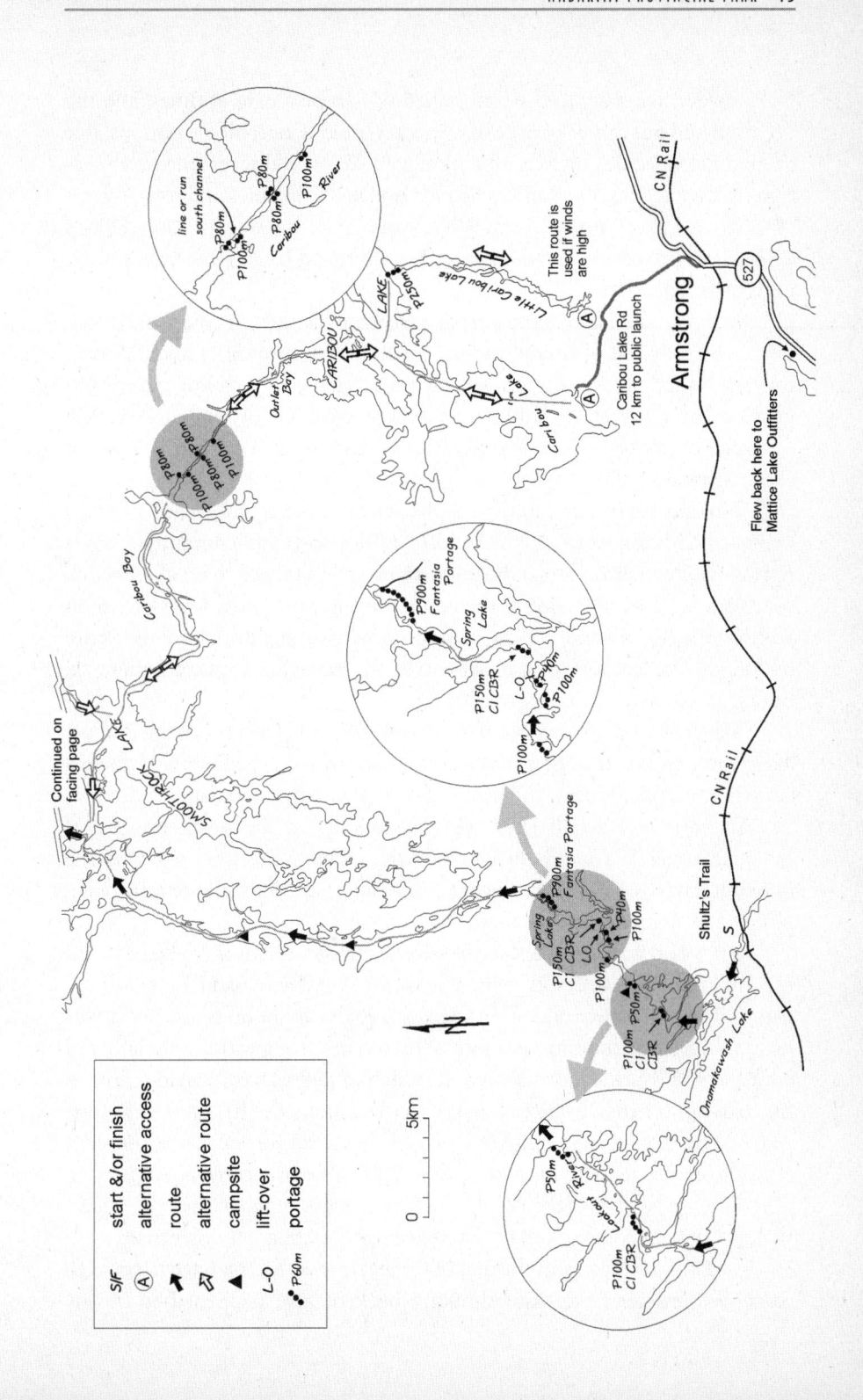

However, keeping to the train schedule can be a pain at times, and the flights in and out can be very costly. So after looking over all the options, our group finally decided on a combination plan. We would access the south section by train (check Via Rail Canada for updated schedules and fees), fly out of Mattice Lake Outfitters on Whitewater Lake by way of Don Elliot's Wabakimi Air Service, and then have Don shuttle us back to the train station in Armstrong.

Since Kip and I live in the Toronto area, we planned to take the Via Rail service directly out of Union Station. Then, if all went well, we would meet up with Nancy twenty-four hours later at the Armstrong station and continue east for another 39 kilometers where we'd be dropped off at the designated access point — Shultz's Trail — at the south end of Onamakawash Lake.

Thinking back, our multi-part plan went surprisingly well. Kip and I managed to bump into only a handful of not-so-polite commuters while portaging down Front Street during rush hour. I managed to break only one overhead light while carrying the canoe through the main foyer of Union Station (which, for some reason, caused a power surge throughout the entire building). And because of a broken axle on the train, we were a mere six hours late to meet Nancy in Armstrong.

Under the watchful eyes of the tourists we had befriended in the Bud car along the way, the three of us waved our good-byes, dragged our gear down a steep gravel embankment, and then paddled off into the Wabakimi wilderness.

An hour and a half later, we had paddled to the northeast bay of Onamakawash Lake and flushed ourselves down the first rapid of the Lookout River (a 100-meter portage is marked to the left), all the time being pursued by a massive black cloud.

Nancy had warned us about the severity of the storms in Wabakimi. But Kip and I thought we could get in at least the first day of paddling before we had to deal with one. Suddenly, the black squall caught up to us. There was no buildup, no prelude, just a smack of hard rain, strong wind, and a lather of whitecaps. We pushed for the second stretch of rapids, hastily made camp at the take-out for the 50-meter portage marked along the left bank, and then watched from under a sagging rain tarp as the storm moved across the sky.

For our second day out, we pushed off from camp early, attempting to film our own version of the Bob Izumi fishing show at the base of the rapids, with no luck, of course. And by 8 a.m. we were heading off downriver.

The Lookout River was the first of three rivers we had planned to travel to reach Whitewater Lake. And thinking back, it also happened to be my favorite. Of the series of five rapids between our first night's camp and Spring Lake, only the fourth could be safely run. But all the portages were extremely short (100 meters on the left, 100 meters and 40 meters on the right, a possible lift-over on the left, and 150 meters on the left), and the scenery along the intimate little stream was absolutely breathtaking. Even the last portage of the day — a 900-meter trail connecting Spring Lake with Smoothrock Lake — was a pleasure to walk. Aptly named Fantasia Portage for its fairyland appearance, and rumored to be the most scenic portage in the north, the trail led us through a stand of pine, spruce and birch, all rooted in a thick carpet of caribou moss, bunchberries and knuckle-size blueberries.

Smoothrock Lake (named for its cluster of islands, scoured smooth by passing glaciers) was a different story, however. Almost the entire 30 kilometers of shoreline had been affected by fire that went through the area in the early 1980s. Since wildfires play an integral part in the lifecycle of the boreal forest, they are not always suppressed here. This management practice ensures a vital habitat for the park's scattered herds of woodland caribou as well as all other boreal species. For canoeists looking for a place to camp, however, the landscape can seem inhospitable. We finally found a suitable spot on a tiny knob of rock situated in the center of the lake around 6 p.m., just minutes before the nightly storm moved in.

It was amazingly calm the next day when we began our six-hour crossing of Smoothrock Lake. On such a large lake, we were grateful for the lack of wind. But the payback was an intense heat, reaching 90 degrees by 8 a.m. We kept close to the shoreline most of the day, searching for a bit of shade. The previous fire had scarred most of the trees along the shore, however, and escaping the direct sun soon became a lost cause. To make matters worse, we could smell smoke from a distant fire, probably lit by a lightning strike from the previous night's storm. Soon, a thin veil of haze hung low over the lake, and breathing became more difficult throughout the day.

By late afternoon, as we entered Smoothrock's Outlet Bay (the second of three channels that lead northward out of the lake), a soft breeze was helping cleanse the air and we were finally free of the smoke. The quick shift in the wind, however, also indicated to us that another evening storm was brewing. In the distance, we spotted anvil-shaped clouds moving our way. This time they had a green hue to them, something Nancy seemed quite concerned about, so we immediately headed for shore.

Of course, as luck would have it, we were quickly chased off by thousands of biting red ants (it was like some kind of horror flick) and we made haste toward the next rocky point. The second we pulled up on shore, the storm hit. And what a storm it was! The temperature dropped 30 degrees in a matter of minutes; hail the size of marbles smacked down hard, leaving dimple marks on the overturned canoes; and a gale-force wind brought trees down all around us.

It was a horrifying experience. But it lasted a mere five minutes. And as we crept out to the water's edge to check the damage done to our two canoes, we realized how lucky we were to make it through the storm without serious injury. The original point we had pulled up on was now a jumbled mess, littered with uprooted trees. It was obvious that if we had stayed there, all three of us might have been crushed to death. It was a humbling experience, to say the least.

The next morning we had only an hour's paddling left on Smoothrock Lake before we reached the portage leading to the Berg River. The trail was only 500 meters long, but this section of forest had been recently burned over and it took us another hour to haul our gear and canoes through the charred debris. Once on the Berg, however, we made quick progress. We easily ran the first set of rapids, even though a short 70-meter portage was marked on the left. The second set, Island Rapids, had to be portaged. But the 80-meter trail along the left bank was an easy carry. Once we reached the third set, we decided to call it an early day and camped along the 400-meter portage, also marked to the left.

Here Kip spent some quality time shooting some whitewater scenes for his film by having me paddle down the Class II–III rapids over half a dozen times. I didn't mind the job, however. The water levels were up and most of the dangerous rocks were well covered. The only thing I had to watch out for was billowing waves at the beginning and end of the run, which became a problem after Kip duct-taped his camera and tripod to the back end of my canoe. With the extra weight strapped to the stern, each maneuver became a balancing act. And since Kip forgot the waterproof casing for the camera, he constantly reminded me that a dump in the rapid would be a costly mistake.

The morning of day five saw us finishing the remainder of the Berg River, and before noon we had entered the Ogoki River. This was the last of the three rivers en route and also happened to be the largest and least exciting to paddle. It's slow and meandering in this section, with only one section of quick water, and that can be easily run or lined down. We also began seeing fishermen from the neighboring lodges. (Wabakimi Provincial Park has seven main lodges and forty fly-in outpost camps.) So, rather than taking the regular 650-meter portage marked to the right of where the main section of the Ogoki empties into Whitewater Lake, we made a sharp left turn a kilometer up from the take-out and navigated a small side stream instead.

There were no portages, and we had to wade, line and blindly run down a series of rock-strewn rapids. But in a way, the narrow outlet was a far better introduction to Whitewater Lake. And there to greet us at the entranceway to Wendell's "Center of the Universe" was our first woodland caribou. The encounter lasted only a couple of seconds, but even the brief glimpse we had was well worth it. Throughout Wabakimi, the second-largest park in the province, only 300 of these elusive creatures remain.

Caribou once ranged as far south as Lake Nipissing, but they were eventually pushed further north by settlement and logging. Because they are an extremely vulnerable species that depends greatly on isolation for its survival, their future viability lies in part here in Wabakimi. The park, established in 1983, was expanded six-fold in 1997, primarily to provide for the protection of the caribou. But is this enough? According to the Ministry of Natural Resources Regional Planning Biologist for Northwestern Ontario, Glen Hooper, it's not even close enough. Hooper admits that the park provides a vast and very significant chuck of habitat for this important population but is not large enough or remote enough to sustain the caribou on its own.

However, the park superintendent, John McGrath, is continuing to promote its high number of hunting and fishing lodges developed throughout its expansion area. Most canoeists traveling in the park feel ambivalent about the camps. In one way they seem intrusive — they don't seem to fit the "wilderness experience." On the other hand, they can be extremely handy as a link to the outside world. Occasionally, trippers use them as a meeting place for floatplanes or to pick up extra supplies. Others have had to use them in severe emergency situations.

Our group was no different. Before our trip to Wabakimi, John McGrath offered to have Walter, the interior park warden, meet us at the lodge situated at the mouth of the Ogoki River. From here he would give us a tow across to the Wendell Beckwith site on Best Island, situated on the far southeast bay of Whitewater Lake — a distance of approximately 20 kilometers.

In a way, it was a bit of a cop-out to accept the free ride. But Walter was also a member of the small group of aboriginal people who lived on Whitewater Lake during Wendell Beckwith's time here, and Kip thought that an interview with him would help his film a great deal. So early the next morning, our group gathered on the lodge's dock and waited for Walter to show. The following day we were still waiting. At 3 a.m. of the second day, the same day we had scheduled a plane to pick us up at another lodge just south of Best Island, we were forced to find our own way across. Of course, when we finally arrived, good old Walter was there to greet us.

Wendell Beckwith's cabin – "The Snail." PHOTO: NANCY SCOTT

After many years of traveling in the north, I've come to realize that schedules are not the same up here as they are down south. I also believe that far too many of us "visitors" have failed to see the importance of not being in such a hurry, and that we should not enter the bush without a good understanding of this. Knowing it, however, didn't seem to help curb my anger toward Walter, and it took some time before we could excuse his tardiness.

To help ease the situation, we went off to explore the splendor of the Wendell Beckwith site. Walter gave us a tour of the three cabins and a couple of storage sheds that still remain on the island, all connected by a flagstone walkway and surrounded by a decorative cedar-rail fence. Each structure was perfectly designed, with every roof shingle and floorboard precisely cut to the same size and shape. Elaborate carving adorned all three entranceways, and pieces of the inventor's scientific contraptions and scores of Ojibwa artifacts were scattered about. Walter even pointed out parts of a homemade telescope he had found down by the beach, and sections of Wendell's "lunar gun" (a device constructed to compute and predict lunar cycles and eclipses) resting beside one of the storage sheds.

The cabins didn't actually belong to Wendell. Harry Wirth, a San Francisco architect and developer, used the island site as a retreat and hired Wendell as a caretaker. In 1955, after producing at least fourteen patents —

most of them for the Parker Pen Company — Wendell left behind a wife and five children in Wisconsin and began his solitary life on Whitewater Lake.

Wendell wasn't the only one to choose Wabakimi as a wilderness retreat. From 1977 to 1982, Joel and Mary Crookham trapped and homesteaded on the nearby Wabakimi Lake and raised their two young children, Sarah and Jason. And in the spring of 1994, Les Stroud and Sue Jamison lived "on what the bush provided" on Goldsborough Lake to work on their film *Snowshoes and Solitude*. Even Zabe, a graduate of Lakehead University's Outdoor Recreation program, attempted to overwinter at Wendell's place. After a close encounter with a pack of wolves, however, she decided to walk back out to Armstrong in February, just five months after she began her sojourn.

But Wendell Beckwith was surely the most unique. During his time here the eccentric inventor worked on various theories, ranging from the idea that the mathematical term "Pi" was constantly reoccurring in nature to the idea that Whitewater Lake was in complete triangulation with the Great Pyramids and Stonehenge (hence the "Center of the Universe" premise).

Obviously, this was no simple hermitage built by a man trying to escape the civilized world; it was a laboratory, observation post and research station.

The first cabin Walter showed us was a split-level building known as the guesthouse, or Rose's Cabin. The modest structure was thought to be the living quarters for Rose Chaltry while she visited Wendell Beckwith. Rose was Harry Wirth's secretary, who came to know Wendell through his letters to Mr. Wirth. Eventually she befriended Wendell and supported him financially after he had a major dispute with Wirth in 1975.

The main cabin, the only structure not completely designed by Beckwith, came with its own ice-box that was lowered underground to keep food from spoiling, and a sizable homemade birchbark canoe lashed to the south wall. This was where Wendell stayed at first, but he soon found it far too showy and impractical. The massive stone fireplace was especially ineffective at heating the cabin during the long winter months, and he became concerned about his reduced hours of research.

By 1978, he had completed construction on the "snail," a circular cabin built directly into the side of a hill. The structure was far more heat-efficient, especially with a skylight centered above a sunken stove, equipped with rotating conical shield to direct the heat and a pivoting chimney to allow for maximum draft. It was an environmental masterpiece, and touring through the unconventional earth-cabin was the highlight of the trip for me.

To end our visit to Best Island, Walter walked us down to the small beach near the Snail and showed us where Wendell died of a heart attack back in

1980, alone but content. It was then that we noticed yet another storm brewing overhead. Since the lodge where we had planned for Don Elliot's air service to pick us up was another 4 kilometers south of Best Island, we made the call to leave immediately.

On cue, good old Walter took off, never offering us a tow, and we hastily went in all directions to complete our different tasks. Nancy prepared the boats, Kip finished filming the interior of the cabins, and I went off to sign our names in the registry book resting on the table inside the Snail. It was here that I saw an entry from Wendell's daughter, Laura, dated August 6, 1997: "Very proud to be the daughter of such a man. Wish everyone could have seen his 'domain' as it was while he was alive. By all accounts he was an exceptional and extraordinary man whose ideas and theories we may never comprehend — but we can all admire what he built here and the life he fashioned for himself. I last hugged him on the beach here — and I feel his presence still. Good bye again, Dad."

Nothing could better have described this charismatic person. Beckwith's "vision" — to have a community of researchers living on the island in their own Snails, "cleansing their minds of the mental paraphernalia in the outside world" — may not have been a bad idea. Truly, he was not some mad scientist, something that Kip and I constantly joked about before our trip here, but a pure Renaissance man who designed a perfect life for himself in this wild place called Wabakimi.

WABAKIMI PROVINCIAL PARK

TIME 8–10 days

NUMBER OF PORTAGES 12

LONGEST PORTAGE 900 meters, Fantasia Portage

DIFFICULTY Although this route includes travel on three separate rivers, the majority of rapids have to be portaged around, and no experience in running whitewater is required. However, Wabakimi's remote setting and its several large lakes make it essential that canoeists have a high level of tripping skills.

ALTERNATIVE ACCESS Rather than access the park by rail or floatplane, you can drive directly to a public launch on Caribou Lake, 12 kilometers north of Armstrong, by way of Armstrong Road (Highway 527) and then Caribou Lake Road. A small parking area, located to the right approximately halfway along Caribou Lake Road, can also be used to access Little Caribou Lake — an alternative route to avoid the more exposed southern half of Caribou Lake.

ALTERNATIVE ROUTE

Smoothrock Lake can be reached by paddling across Caribou Lake (use Little Caribou Lake if winds are too high) to Outlet Bay and then down the Caribou River to Caribou Bay. Then, once you've followed the regular route to Whitewater Lake's Best Island, you can loop back to Smoothrock Lake by heading south through McKinley Lake, Laurent Lake and Smoothrock's Lonebreast Bay. From here you then backtrack on the Caribou River and Caribou Lake.

OUTFITTERS

MATTICE LAKE OUTFITTERS AND AIR SERVICE
Box 157
Armstrong, Ontario
P0T 1A0
807-583-2483
www.duenorth.net/matticelake/location.htm

WILDWATERS NATURE TOURS AND EXPEDITIONS LTD.
RR 14, Dog Lake Rd.
Thunder Bay, Ontario
P7B 5E5
807-767-2022

or
Frontier Trail, Hwy. 527
Armstrong, Ontario
P0T 1A0
807-583-2626
e-mail: forests@tbaytel.net
www.wabakimi.com/wildwaters

SMOOTHROCK CAMPS
Box 278
Armstrong, Ontario
P0T 1A0
807-583-2617 (summer)
807-623-8542 (winter)
www.smoothrock.com

FOR MORE INFORMATION

Park Superintendent
WABAKIMI PROVINCIAL PARK
Ontario Parks
435 James St. S.
Suite 221d
Thunder Bay, Ontario
P7E 6S8
807-475-1634
www.wabakimi.on.ca/wabakimi

VIA RAIL CANADA
1-888-VIARAIL (1-888-842-7245)
www.viarail.ca

TOPOGRAPHIC MAPS

52 I/6, 52 I/11, 52 I/12, 52 I/14 & 53 I/5

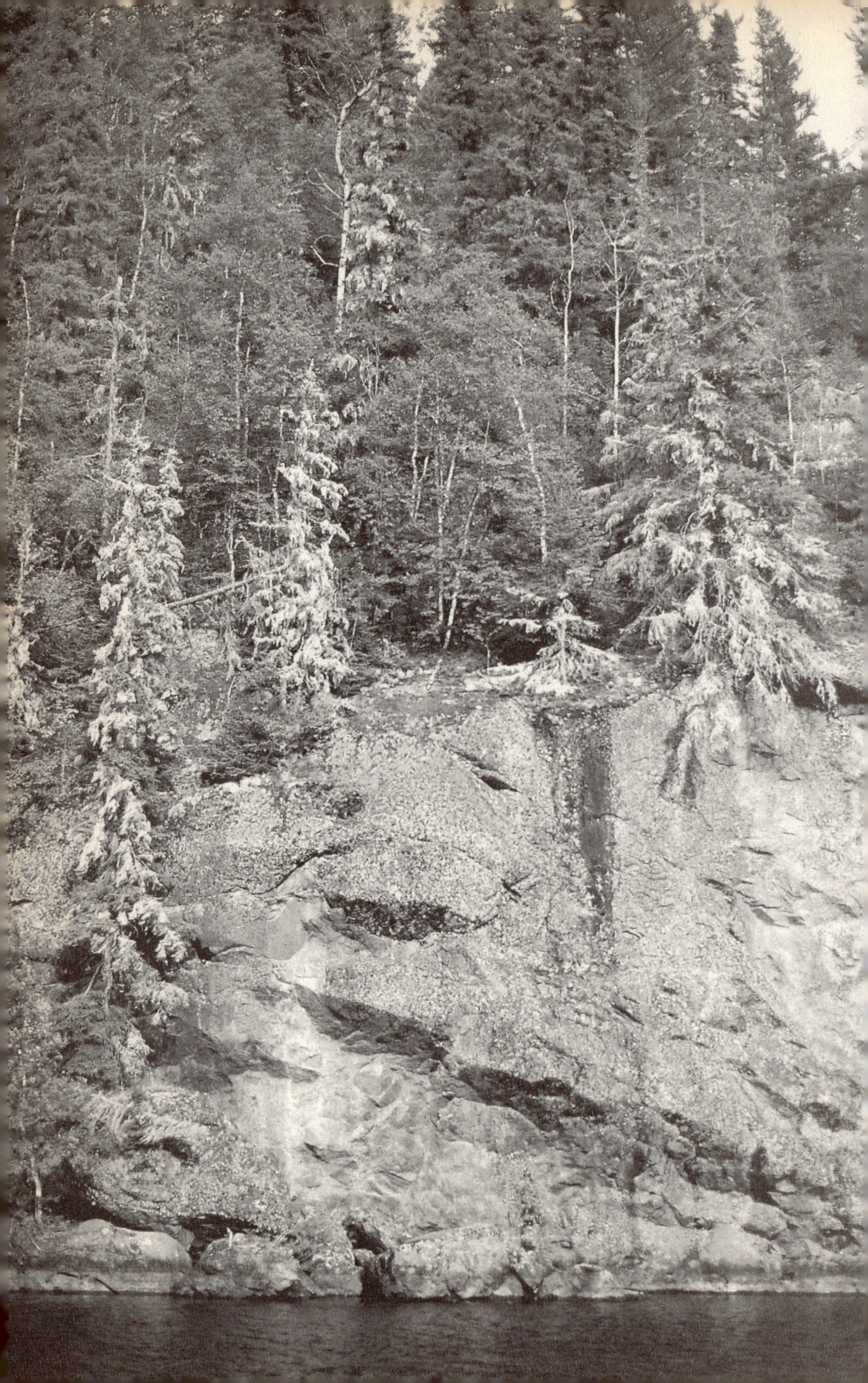

STEEL RIVER LOOP

IT WAS DIFFICULT TO BELIEVE that the almost sheer slab of rock directly in front of us was actually the beginning of the Diablo Portage. It was not as if my wife and I thought that a wilderness trail named after Lucifer would be a walk in the park. In fact, everything Alana and I had heard and read before heading out on the Steel River, north of Lake Superior, had given us good reason to avoid this 1,000-meter portage, which immediately begins with a 350-meter rise in elevation.

In most cases, canoeists will choose to use a logging road north of Terrace Bay to access the main section of the river, reducing a ten-day trip to only five days and, at the same time, avoiding some of the most rugged topography en route. If you take the easy way out, however, you also have to organize a lengthy car shuttle — the plague of most river routes, one that I desperately try to avoid — instead of looping directly back to your vehicle. And besides, our pre-trip research also indicated that the first few days of the full 170-kilometer circuit allowed canoeists to travel through some of the most scenic landscape the province has to offer. Alana and I figured such a large chunk of wilderness was well worth portaging through hell and back and decided to take on the infamous Diablo Portage despite the warnings of canoeists who had gone before us. After all, how bad could one portage really be?

The original access point for the Steel River Loop was the rail bridge close to the shore of Lake Superior. (Canadian Pacific Railway brochures of the 1890s advertised this route as a prime canoe destination.) But now canoeists use the government dock at the south end of Santoy Lake, located at the end of a gravel road leading in from Highway 17, 4.6 kilometers west

One of the many spectacular cliff faces found along the downstream run of the Steel River.

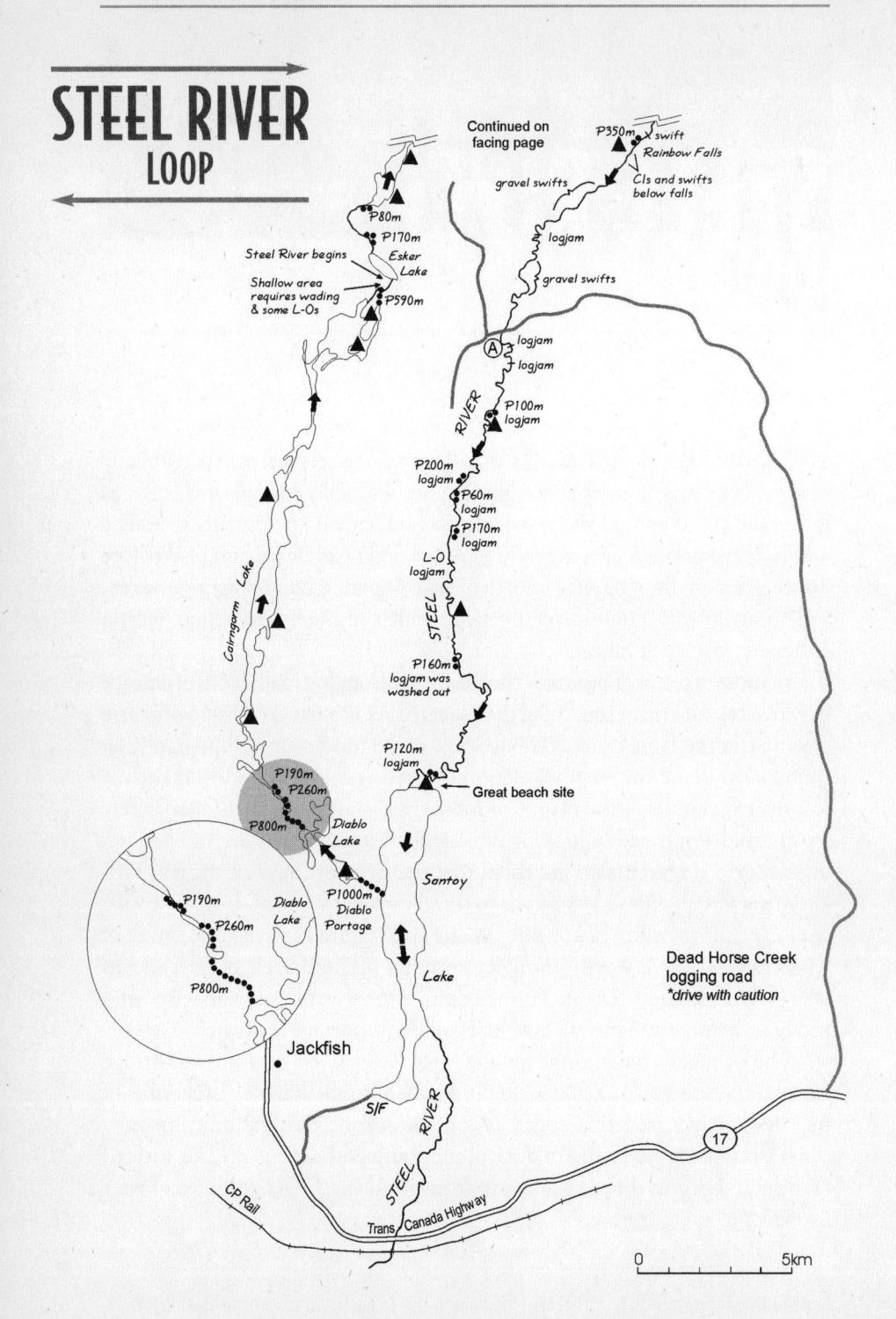

STEEL RIVER
LOOP

Continued on facing page

P350m — swift
Rainbow Falls
Cls and swifts below falls
gravel swifts
logjam
gravel swifts

P80m
P170m
Steel River begins
Esker Lake
Shallow area requires wading & some L-Os
P590m

A
logjam
logjam
P100m logjam

STEEL RIVER

P200m logjam
P60m logjam
P170m logjam
L-O logjam

Cairngorm Lake

P160m logjam was washed out

P120m logjam
Great beach site

P190m
P260m
P800m
Diablo Lake

P1000m Diablo Portage

Santoy Lake

Inset:
P190m
P260m
Diablo Lake
P800m

Jackfish

S/F

STEEL RIVER

Dead Horse Creek logging road
*drive with caution

17

CP Rail
Trans Canada Highway

0 5km

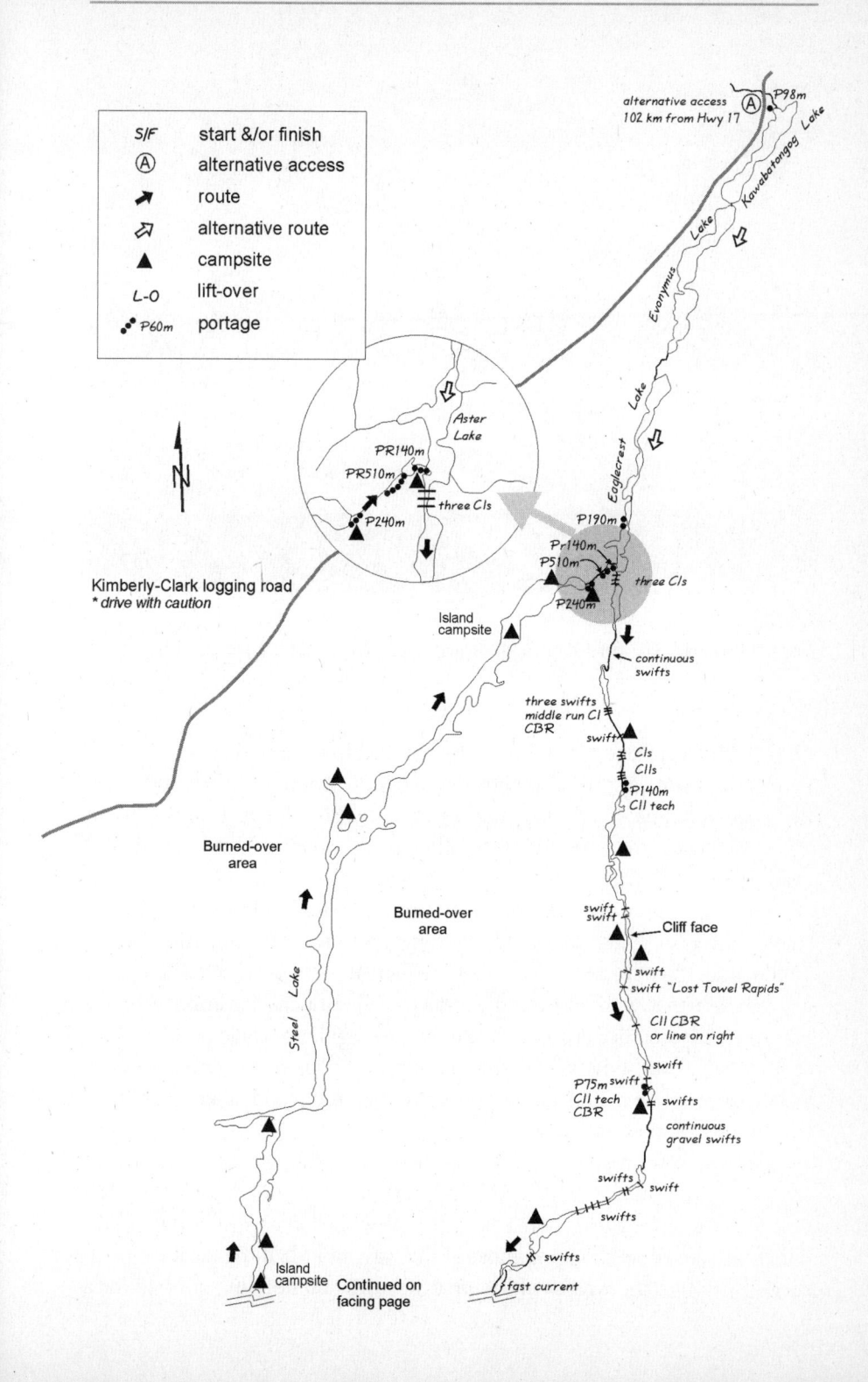

STEEL RIVER LOOP 25

"Are we there yet?" Alana and I search for the portage leading toward Cairngorm Lake.

of the highway bridge. The take-out for the Diablo Portage is actually 8 kilometers north on Santoy Lake, between two high mounds of rock and along the west shoreline. It's poorly marked by a strip of blue ribbon tied to an alder branch and the letter P spray-painted on the weathered trunk of an old cedar tree.

Our plan was to first haul our canoe and gear up the almost vertical section of the trail. Once we had everything up to the summit, Alana and I would then double-carry over what remained — a somewhat level but rugged path that worked through a steep-walled ravine for approximately 800 meters. It sounded reasonable. But on any regular portage, walking with at least half your body weight strapped tight to your back is no easy task. Pulling yourself up a 30-degree slope, with loose rocks and fallen trees littering the path, is closer to suicide.

Somehow we managed to get the first two packs up. Even our hyper Springer spaniel, Bailey, coped with lugging her ten days of dog kibble to the top. On the second trip, Alana had to deal with the largest of our packs, which she ended up dragging most of the way, and I had the darn canoe to carry. Although the weight of the boat was only 60 pounds (not bad for a plastic model), I felt uneasy blindly walking up a rock ledge with it balancing over my head.

I cursed a lot at first, hoping the profanity would give me some type of superhuman strength to help me along. But I finally had to give in about halfway. At this point the bow of the canoe was continuously ramming into the trail in front of me. Any forward motion became impossible and I had to resort to winching the canoe uphill by looping a rope around a solid tree at the top of the rise.

An hour later, Alana, Bailey and I had somehow successfully gathered everything to the top without serious injury. Thinking the worst was over, we immediately continued on to Diablo Lake. Little did we know the worst was yet to come.

It was apparent the trail had not been maintained for quite some time, as the correct path was extremely difficult to locate. Even when an obvious route was laid out in front of us, it was blocked either by a pile of jagged boulders or fallen trees. A network of well-hidden crevices also made walking with a full load of gear extremely hazardous.

Surprisingly, by the time the portage was completed we had had to deal with only three major mishaps: I fell into one of the trip holes and had the canoe come crashing down on me, leaving a large gash on my forehead; Alana took a tumble and managed to wedge her face between two sharp rocks (we renamed the trail Face-Plant Portage after the incident); and Bailey had a close encounter with a wild lynx while she rushed ahead of us on the portage (she's been afraid of our neighbor's cat ever since).

It took us half the day to complete the dreaded trip across Diablo, and once out on the lake we took the first campsite — a small island stuck out in the middle of the west bay. The three of us dragged our gear up to the site and, wherever we happened to collapse, Alana, Bailey and I took time out for a well-deserved snooze before cooking up dinner.

Obviously we were slow to start the next day. It wasn't until 10 a.m. that we began taking on the first of three consecutive portages leading into Cairngorm Lake. Fortunately the trail wasn't as steep as Diablo. But at times it seemed just as demanding. It measured a long 800 meters and, thanks again to poor maintenance over the years, the proper trail was extremely difficult to locate. The worst part, however, was getting to the put-in. For some reason the trail ended early, at least 200 meters away from the next lake, and Alana and I had to push our way through a bug-infested marsh to reach open water.

The second portage, found to the right of a small creek and measuring a seemingly long 260 meters, was easier to find but extremely wet in places.

And once again a number of downed trees cluttered the path and turned what should have been a relatively easy carry-over into a frustrating and dangerous ordeal.

The take-out for the third portage (190 meters) was the most challenging to find. A beaver dam had covered the first section, and Alana and I searched both sides of the creek for half an hour before we discovered a faint path crossing over from right to left only 30 meters from the dam.

Eventually we reached Cairngorm Lake and were lucky enough to have a tail wind for the entire 16-kilometer crossing. Of course, with the south wind came rain. So rather than set up camp early on one of the islands clumped together at the far end of the lake, Alana and I decided to continue on to Steel Lake.

Cairngorm's far northern bay is where the Steel River begins, flushing itself over a moderate falls found at the northern tip of the lake. The portage, however, is nowhere near the falls. To reach the take-out for the 590-meter carry, you have to paddle to the far end of the northeast bay.

It's a surprisingly easy trail, at least when compared to what Alana and I had already endured. But the narrow stretch of river below the cascade was a different story. From here to Esker Lake we walked most of the way, wading over shallow riffles and lifting over several logjams blocking the stream.

Once on Esker Lake (an extremely scenic spot) we were forced to pull up on a beach along the north shore and spend some time orienting ourselves. The pamphlet supplied by the government made no sense here. It told of another portage (measuring 170 meters and to the right of another cascade) at the far end of Esker Lake. The portage didn't exist, however, until at least another kilometer downriver, which made us second-guess everything the map told us from here on in.

It was quite late by the time we hauled all our gear over yet another rough carry-over. To make matters worse, it still was raining. And after consulting the map, we knew there was at least another hour of river paddling ahead, plus another portage to deal with (80 meters and marked to the right of a small chute). By the looks of things, we would be setting up camp on the lower half of Steel Lake just before dark — cold, wet and very hungry.

Alana and I weren't all that concerned, though. It wouldn't be the first time we had to cook dinner in the dark. Besides, we were slowly getting used to roughing it. And by now, we were beginning to reap our rewards for paddling in such a remote place. That afternoon we had spotted two bald eagles, a family of otter, and a cow moose with twin calves — proof that the Steel is truly a wild place.

"The portage has to be here somewhere." Alana leads the way through an old burn.

Alana and I crawled out of the tent the next morning feeling a little anxious about the coming day's events. We had to cross the entire 30 kilometers of Steel Lake, which happens to be perfectly lined up with the prevailing winds. We also had to assume that the scenery wouldn't be all that exciting throughout the day, since most of Steel Lake's shoreline was burned to a crisp by a forest fire only two years earlier. Thinking back, though, paddling across this gigantic lake was actually a highlight of the trip. We were lucky enough to have a south wind help us down the lake and we made camp near the north end as early as 2:30 p.m. Seeing the effects of the fire was also a much more positive experience than we had expected. The new plant life growing thick beneath the blackened stumps was a true sign of how diverse this rugged landscape was. As well, only the tops of the ridges were severely scarred. Less exposed areas, where either stands of poplar and birch indicated deeper soil or where the fire had burned at night when the wind was down, proved how highly local a wildfire actually is.

The only negative part of the day was that it continued to rain down hard on us, especially when we stopped to make camp. Our site was on a small island that had little cover and the rain tarp had to be set up away from the firepit. At first we would snuggle up under the tarp and then head over to the fire between bursts of rain to try and dry ourselves out. It wasn't long, however, before the constant drizzle put out our fire and the cold wind made sitting under the tarp unbearable. So we escaped to the tent and spent the night curled up in our sleeping bags, reading the books we'd packed along: Alana had chosen *A Walk in the Woods* by Bill Bryson and I had *The Tent Dwellers* by Albert Bigalow Paine. Reading about someone else's misadventures in the wilderness helped make our trip seem less of a disaster.

The storm continued through the night, and come morning it was difficult to leave the warmth of the sleeping bags to cook breakfast out in the rain. Actually, we had no need to get up early since the continuous south wind had left us at least two days ahead of schedule. But we were only three portages away from Aster Lake — the turnaround point of the trip — and were looking forward to beginning the river section.

It took us only an hour to pack up and paddle the remainder of Steel Lake. It was another two hours, however, before we'd finished the three portages leading to Aster Lake.

The first and third portage (240 meters and 140 meters, marked on the right) were relatively easy. It was on the second portage (510 meters and also marked on the right) that we spent most of our time. The trail worked its way alongside a steep ravine, where getting a good foothold was at times next to impossible. The ridge we were walking along had also been heavily burned over and, besides the normal problem of downed trees blocking the path, big patches of blueberry and raspberry bushes hid large sections of the trail.

It was beyond doubt that the entire area was a perfect feeding ground for black bears (we counted four piles of fresh bear scat directly at the take-out), and I actually considered lining the rapids instead. A quick look at the strength of the water being flushed through the chasm, however, confirmed that battling bear phobia along the portage would be far less stressful. We walked the trail making as much noise as possible.

Returning to the take-out for the second load, I spotted bear tracks beside our food barrel, tracks that weren't there before. I was amazed that nothing had been disturbed. His gait was straight, not irregular, and went directly toward a patch of ripe blueberries. The bear had obviously ignored whatever temptations our freeze-dried foods provided. (Having eaten the stuff for the previous four days, I couldn't blame him in the least.)

Eventually we reached Aster Lake, turned south, and almost immediately began running rapids. The whitewater was a welcome diversion. Only once did we have to portage, 140 meters to the left of a technical Class II rapid. The rest of the day was spent negotiating a combination of fast chutes, manageable Class Is, and easy swifts. In fact, the strong current remained consistent most of the way, squeezing itself through walls of granite or high gravel banks. Even when the river eventually broadened out, becoming more lake-like, the scenery still remained breathtaking. Jagged cliffs provided a backdrop to thick-forested banks, left untouched by the fire, and tiny islands of sand and gravel split the current in all directions. It was a place of awesome beauty, an absolute dreamscape.

We camped directly across from a spectacular cliff-face, and celebrated the day with an extra glass of wine. It continued to pour down rain while we set up camp, but at this point in the day nothing seemed to dampen our spirits. Even when Alana discovered we were missing two very important items from our pack — a bottle of biodegradable soap and our second roll of toilet paper — we calmly planned out a strategy. I replaced the soap with alcohol swabs from the first-aid kit and Alana began reading her paperback novel to provide surplus T.P.

Our second day on the river was just as exciting as the first. We spent a good part of the morning fishing between two swifts and caught a mess of walleye and pike. We also successfully ran two technical Class II rapids. Neither of them was marked on our map. But then again, none of the rapids were, and we were now used to checking out each and every bend in the river.

The first Class II was approximately 2 kilometers down from the last swift. It looked possible to line along the right bank, but Alana and I chose to run straight through. The only disappointment was that we had forgotten to put away the towel Alana had left on top of the packs to dry and so had to name the set Lost Towel Rapids.

After already misplacing the soap and extra toilet paper during the trip, we thought losing the towel was quite a big deal — until we noticed a collection of someone else's camping gear washed up at the base of the rapid. One noticeable item was a T-shirt reading "I'm not as think as you drunk I am."

Before our trip the tourist office in Terrace Bay informed us that a group of local canoeists paddling the river in early May had dumped in some rapids. They were able to retrieve one canoe and two members paddled out for help. Eventually a helicopter retrieved the other canoeists but left all their gear behind — including a favorite T-shirt, I guess.

Two kilometers downstream from Lost Towel Rapids were two more swifts and just beyond them was the second technical Class II rapid.

We checked the run from a rough 75-meter portage on the right and, after making the decision to attempt it, rushed back to the canoe and pushed

Rainbow Falls is one of the high points of paddling the remote Steel River.

off from shore. Just before the drop I stood up to re-check our predetermined route while Alana gave Bailey the command to sit (the one thing our dog is good at is sitting still during rapids). It was all over quickly, and even though we took a totally different route than the one we had planned, only the stack of high waves at the end caused some concern. But we were able to slow the boat down just before smacking into the haystacks and kept most of the water out.

A quick current continued almost right up to the brink of Rainbow Falls. Here, the river opens up just ahead of the 20-meter drop, and Alana and I inched our canoe slowly toward the take-out for the 350-meter portage on the right.

It's a good trail around the falls, except for a steep section past the campsite marked three-quarters of the way along. The site is also well away from the water, and Alana and I chose to have our lunch break back near the take-out instead.

A good set of rapids begins immediately beyond the falls, with some sections that are even quite technical. But eventually the river leaves Shield country and its current tires out. The banks begin to meander uncontrollably, the water turns murky with silt, and any evidence of mountainous rock can be seen only in brief, distant glimpses.

A good number of logs were also beginning to block our path. Alana and I had to either walk around them, sinking up to our knees in the silty mud deposited along the shore, or lift directly over them, always being careful not to go broadside with the current.

Our map indicated where we had to actually portage around a total of five massive logjams later in the route. But soon after passing under a logging bridge, Alana and I came to a giant buildup of logs that had obviously been formed since the map was printed.

Neither side of the river showed any evidence of a portage, so, for no real reason, we chose to get out on the left bank. Then I volunteered to get out of the canoe, scramble up the 4-meter-high bank, and search the shore for a way around the jam. Alana stayed behind to prevent our hyper dog, Bailey, from following me into the bush. Bailey is the greatest canoe-tripping dog, and can actually find a portage better than I can. But she tries my patience at times, and this was not the moment for her to run into another lynx.

The second I entered the brush I hit a wall of deadfall. The best I could do was detour away from the eroded bank, and head deeper and deeper into the woods. But there was still no apparent trail.

Just when I was about to call it quits and suggest to Alana that we paddle back to the logging road and thumb a ride, I looked down and spotted a Tootsie Roll wrapper. Usually when I see garbage left behind in the forest, I curse the thoughtless person who dropped it there. Now I thanked them. They had left a piece of encouragement, a bit of proof that someone else had actually made it around — and survived. I hurried back, and Alana and I began the ordeal of dragging our gear through an entanglement of fallen trees and dense vegetation.

The distance we covered was only 100 meters. The time it took us to haul everything up the incredibly steep bank, cut a trail with our flimsy camp-saw, and follow it through like a couple of out-of-shape limbo contestants, was an insane two hours and five minutes.

It was 7 p.m. by the time we stopped for the day, and the second we made camp a violent thunderstorm forced us into the confines of the tent. Our site was a small sand spit, as vulnerable as any place could possibly be, and at times we could actually feel the lightning strike the ground around us. But our weariness overpowered any fear we had of the chaos going on outside and we soon passed out with exhaustion.

Around midnight I crawled out of the tent to pee. The storm had moved on by then, leaving a clear evening sky and a welcome calm. I took a short walk barefoot along the beach, relieved myself, and then sat down by the water to listen to two barred owls conversing with one another across the river. What a beautiful setting. This small, intimate river has so much to offer; it was just a matter of getting my mind set on the good points rather than the bad. So before crawling back into bed, I promised myself to have a more positive attitude toward whatever was waiting for us downstream.

Of course, come morning only a short twenty-minute paddle brought us to the next logjam. It was bigger than the first, and the 200-meter portage that was supposed to be marked on the right bank had been completely washed out. It was raining again, and the moment we stepped out of the canoe, mosquitoes swarmed us by the thousands. Trying to remain positive, however, I allowed Bailey to go first this time to scout out a trial. And after considerable deliberation, she actually discovered a somewhat clear path around the worst of it. This time we were back on the river in less than an hour.

Another hour downstream was a third logjam, complete with a rough 60-meter path on the left, and not far beyond was a fourth. This one was the largest yet, reaching at least 5 meters in height. The good news was that it actually had a marked portage (170 meters) on the left. A new collection of logs had blocked the initial take-out, adding another 50 meters to the trail, but it still was quite an easy carry, considering.

This was definitely a sign of better things to come, and we pushed on with more vigor than ever before. By noon we were paddling "through" the next pile of logs. Our map indicated a 160-meter portage on the right. Luckily, however, the entire blockage had been pushed aside by spring floodwaters.

Another two and a half hours of leisurely river paddling brought us to the last logjam (this one measured at least 7 meters high), complete with a clear 120-meter portage on the right, and eventually, the entrance to Santoy Lake.

Santoy is an enormous strip of blue reaching far off to the south and is bordered by huge mounds of granite. It's a place of incredible beauty but can also become extremely dangerous when the wind picks up. There was only a slight breeze when we arrived, and Alana and I even considered taking advantage of the calm to paddle the last 12 kilometers to the launch site that evening. One look at the gigantic beach stretching out across the entire north end of the lake, however, and we couldn't resist spending one more night out.

Our decision was, in hindsight, foolhardy. We began the crossing as early as 5:30 a.m. but by 6 a.m. we were bailing water out of the canoe about every fifth stroke.

To help beat the wind, Alana and I kept close to the west shore. It was the same rugged shoreline that held the dreadful Diablo Portage, and the high cliffs did little to protect us from the rough water. Rebounding waves slapped back from the rock and constantly tossed our canoe broadside to the wind.

I began shouting out, yelling obscenities at the wind, the rock, and the gulping waves. It was fatigue that was making me overreact. I guess we were destined to end the trip just as we had begun — in absolute fear. After all, isn't that what wilderness canoeing is all about? A painful, nerve-racking ordeal mixed together with the most peaceful, uplifting and self-satisfying thing you've ever done.

STEEL RIVER LOOP

TIME 8–10 days

NUMBER OF PORTAGES 16

LONGEST PORTAGE 1,000 meters, Diablo Portage

DIFFICULTY Only intermediate whitewater skills are needed for the river section of the trip. However, you must have advanced canoe-tripping skills because of the remoteness of the entire route. Canoeists must also be physically fit to deal with the demands of most portages.

ALTERNATIVE ACCESS Kawabatongog Lake, approximately 100 kilometers' drive north of Terrace Bay on the Kimberly Clark Road, and at Deadhorse Creek Road bridge crossing, approximately 35 kilometers north of Highway 17.

ALTERNATIVE ROUTE To avoid the entire lake section of the trip as well as the difficult Diablo Portage, use the Kawabatongog Lake access for a five-day trip down the Steel River. Deadhorse Creek Road bridge crossing can also be used to eliminate all the logjams on the lower section of the river.

OUTFITTERS

JACKFISH LAKE MOTEL & EFFICIENCY COTTAGES
Box 436
Terrace Bay, Ontario
P0T 2W0
807-825-9293

FOR MORE INFORMATION

STEEL RIVER PROVINCIAL PARK
Box 970
Nipigon, Ontario
P0T 2J0
807-887-5010

TOPOGRAPHIC MAPS

42 D/15, 42 E/2 & 42 E/7

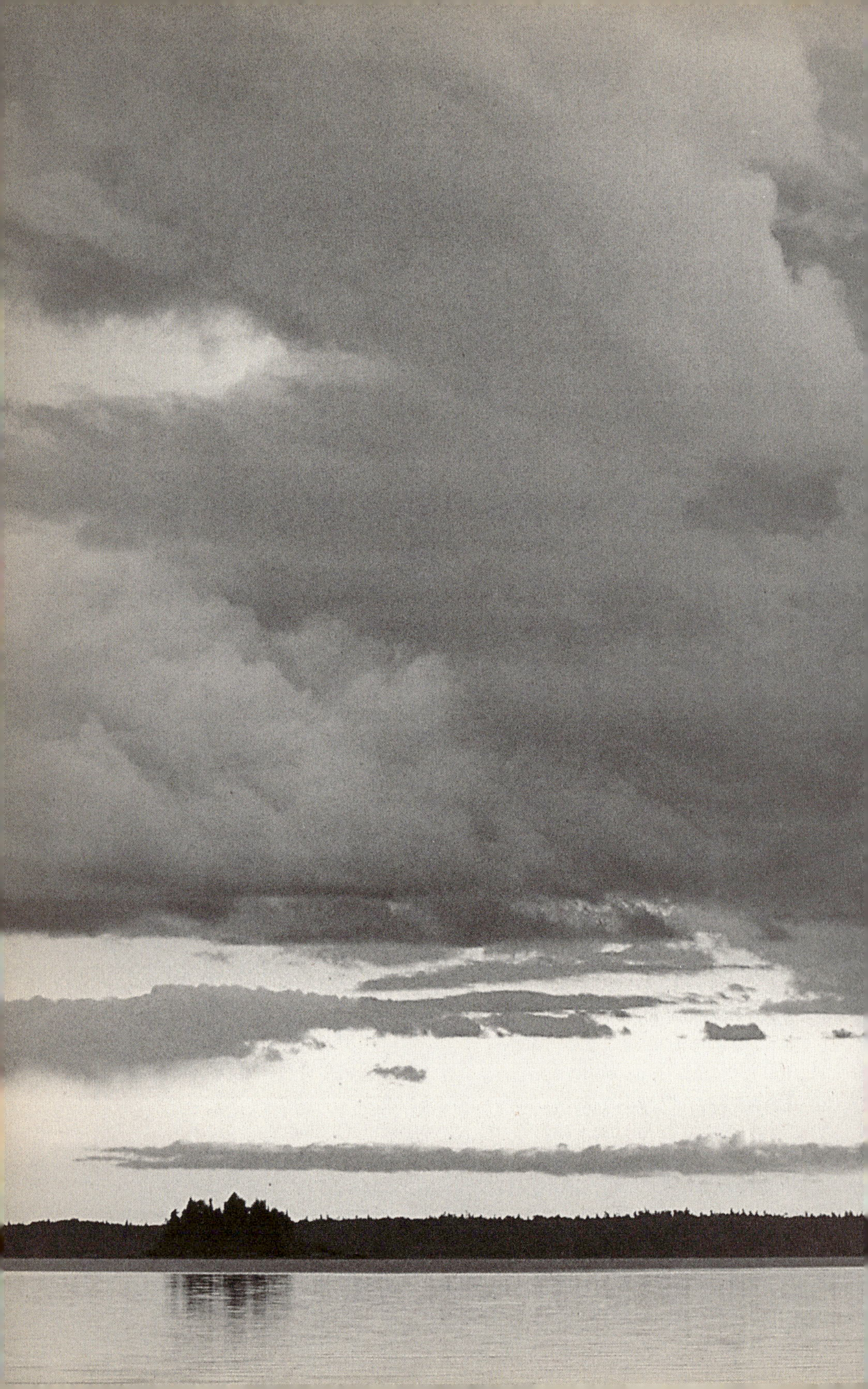

CHAPLEAU AND NEMEGOSENDA RIVERS

COMPARED TO OTHER SCENIC CANOE ROUTES located in the north, the Chapleau-Nemegosenda Waterway Park doesn't have the same appeal as places such as the Missinaibi River or Temagami. Nor is it as remote as Wabakimi Provincial Park or Lake Superior's Steel River. What it does have, however, is accessibility. There are countless ways to paddle it, from a leisurely five-day jaunt down either river to a full twelve-day, 206-kilometer circuit beginning and ending in the town of Chapleau. Whatever route you happen to choose, you need only a moderate level of experience.

My wife, Alana, and I chose an eight-day route beginning at Racine Lake and ending just north of Highway 101. We weren't going to complete a full loop but we would eliminate the busiest section around the town of Chapleau and take full advantage of the outfitting and shuttle facilities provided at Missinaibi Headwaters, located on Racine Lake. The outfitters even operate a campground on the west shore of the lake, making it a great place to spend the night before heading out.

Most of our first morning out was spent paddling on Racine Lake and then making our way down Racine Creek to the Chapleau River. Traveling the creek took just a quarter of that time, because it had only two portages, easy ones — one at the beginning (100 meters and marked to the right) and a second at the end (240 meters and also marked on the right) — and a shallow section to be lifted over in between. It was the lake itself that was far more time-consuming. The most direct route to the far east bay, where Racine Creek empties out of the lake, was to head straight across from the outfitter's beach. And even though we were on the water early, a stiff morning breeze made traversing the shallow lake extremely difficult.

Sunset on Kapuskasing Lake.

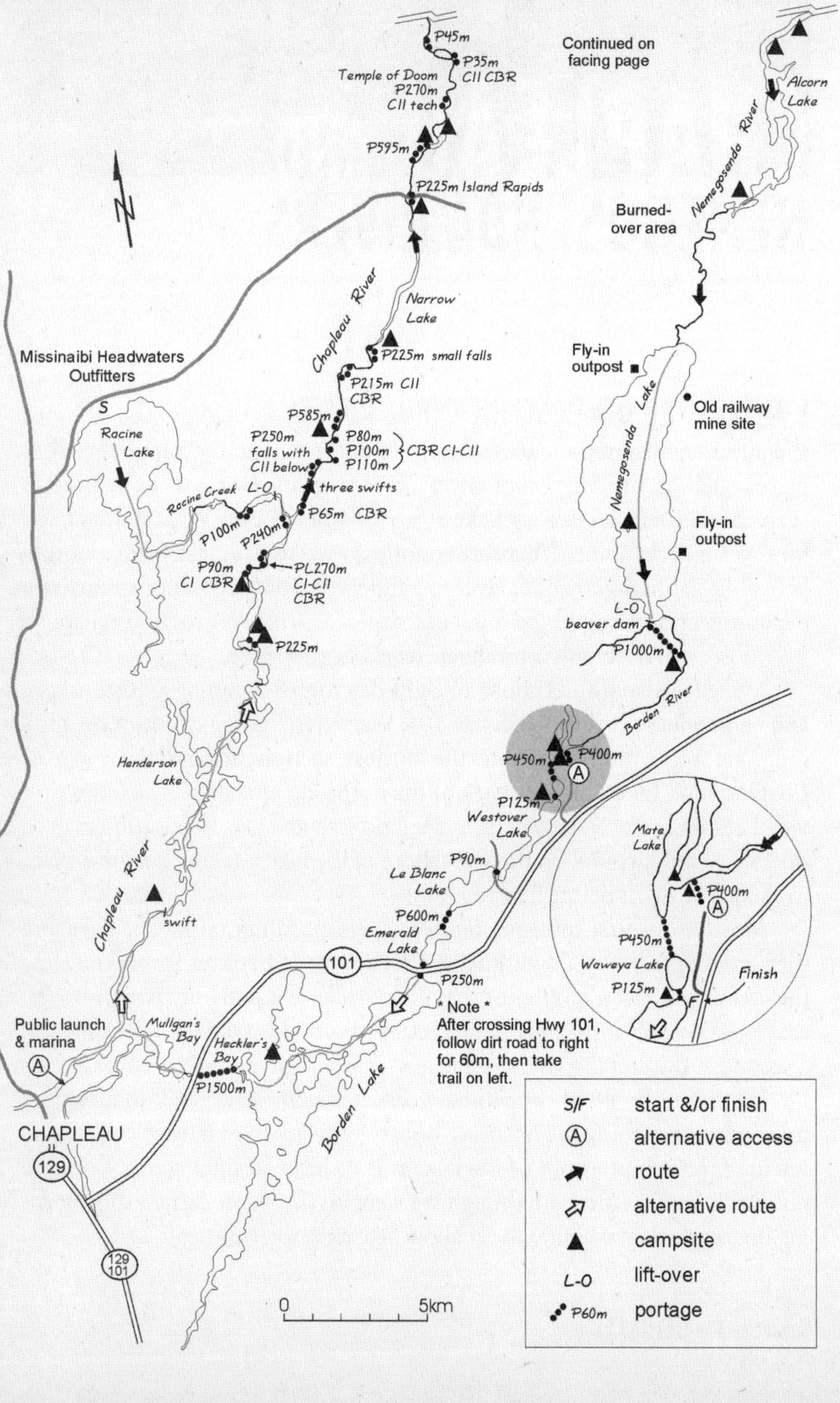

Continued on facing page
P45m
P35m
CII CBR
Temple of Doom
P270m
CII tech
P595m
P225m Island Rapids
Alcorn Lake
Nemegosenda River
Burned-over area
Chapleau River
Narrow Lake
P225m small falls
Missinaibi Headwaters Outfitters
P215m CII CBR
Fly-in outpost
Nemegosenda Lake
Old railway mine site
S
Racine Lake
P585m
P250m falls with CII below
P80m
P100m
P110m
CBR CI-CII
three swifts
Racine Creek
L-O
P65m CBR
P100m
P240m
Fly-in outpost
P90m CI CBR
PL270m CI-CII CBR
L-O beaver dam
P225m
P1000m
Borden River
Henderson Lake
P450m
P400m
P125m
Westover Lake
Mate Lake
P90m
Le Blanc Lake
Chapleau River
swift
P600m
Emerald Lake
P400m
P450m
Waweya Lake
P125m
F
Finish
101
P250m
* Note *
After crossing Hwy 101, follow dirt road to right for 60m, then take trail on left.
Public launch & marina
Mullgan's Bay
Heckler's Bay
P1500m
Borden Lake
CHAPLEAU
129
129
101
0
5km
S/F start &/or finish
A alternative access
route
alternative route
campsite
L-O lift-over
P60m portage

CHAPLEAU AND NEMEGOSENDA RIVERS 39

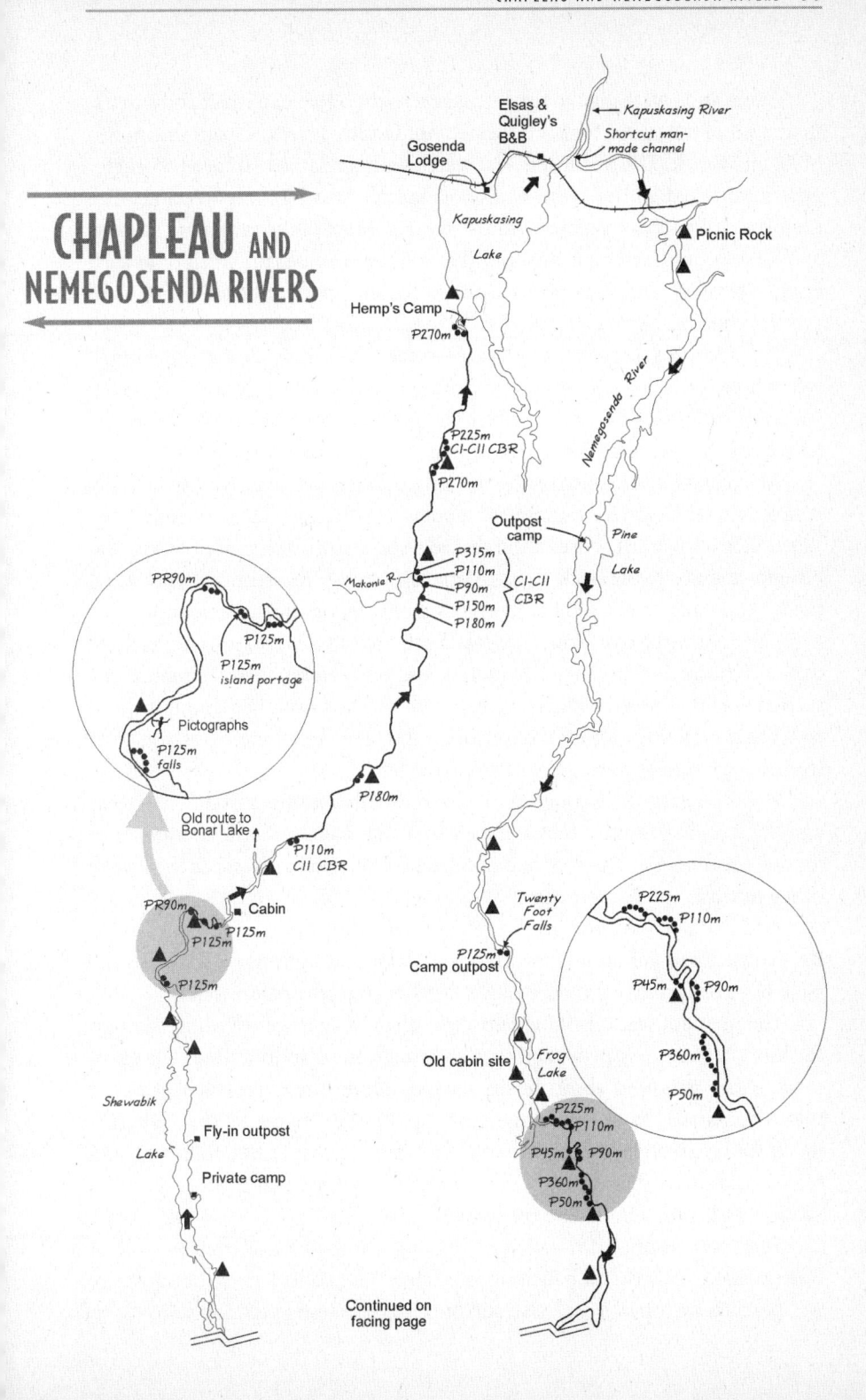

Alana and I were glad to finally make it to the Chapleau River and run the first rapid of the route, which is located not far downstream from the mouth of Racine Creek. This section of fast water, with a relatively unused 65-meter portage marked to the right, is a good sample of what was to come. The Chapleau River is not a major whitewater trip. Most of the rapids are shallow and full of boulders. But a large number of them can be run, lined or at least easily portaged, and they provide an excellent opportunity for paddlers to practise their wilderness tripping skills in relative safety.

The second section of whitewater is soon to follow. After a few quick swifts, the take-out of a 250-meter portage marks the beginning of a small waterfall and a set of Class II rapids. The portage must be used to avoid the falls, but expert canoeists can run or line the rapids below the falls.

Alana and I carried across the full length of the portage. We had actually planned on taking on the rapids below, but when our dog, Bailey, ran down the side trail leading to the base of the cascade, she disturbed a nest of wasps and brought them directly back to us. Alana was stung three times. I was stung twice. And Bailey had a total of five nasty stings, all on the tip of her nose.

The next three consecutive rapids, each having a rough portage marked to the right (at 110 meters, 100 meters and 80 meters), were runnable; the second was the most challenging. A fourth set, however, had enough sharp rocks scattered throughout it to seriously damage our canoe. So Alana and I took the 585-meter portage marked on the left.

It was an extremely rough trail, blocked with a number of downed trees and thick undergrowth. In fact, the entire route had seen little maintenance for quite some time. The distance also seemed off. (I actually paced the length of the portage at 850 meters.)

And, believe it or not, while we made our way though the thick brush, Bailey disturbed yet another wasp nest. Alana and I got more stings to the back of our exposed legs and Bailey's face became covered in welts.

The incident was absolutely unsettling. After years of traveling through the bush, we've never provoked so many wasps in so short a time. The event made us so paranoid about bushwhacking along the overgrown portages that Alana and I chose to line the next rapid rather than take the easy 215-meter trail marked on the right bank. And on the portage that followed (225 meters and marked to the right of a small cascade), we made our way across cautiously, keeping Bailey on the leash.

Then we stopped for the day, making camp on the bottom end of Narrow Lake. It wasn't a bad spot to pitch a tent, considering the campsite was perched on top of a rock slab surrounded by marsh grass. Sadly, however,

Campsite on Narrow Lake, Chapleau River.

the canoeists who had used the site before us had left it a mess. Garbage was piled up everywhere. Worst of all, a number of toilet-paper mounds were left only a few meters back from the tent pad. I even noticed human feces floating in the river, close to the shoreline.

The next site was only a short paddle across Narrow Lake, at the take-out of another portage, but our map showed a logging road directly beside it and we figured it would be just as dirty as the one we were already on. So we made the best of it by burning the garbage and T.P. in a very hot fire, paddled out in the river to collect our water that evening, and planned to leave the site as early as possible come morning.

Our predawn departure the next day was rewarded when we had the chance to spot an osprey dive-bombing a two-pound walleye and then watched as a mature bald eagle attempted to steal the fish the second the osprey had plucked it from the water. When we pulled up at the take-out for the portage adjacent to the logging road, Alana and I confirmed that the site was just a filthy as where we had stayed. It was also occupied by another canoeist, John Mitchell, who was traveling the entire 206-kilometer loop solo.

After Alana and I introduced ourselves, John informed us that his site was actually not as polluted as ours, at least it wasn't until a group of local anglers gave him a visit just before nightfall. The fishermen quickly became inebriated and extremely rowdy, but eventually left John alone after trashing the place with their empty beer cans and fish guts. Needless to say, he was happy to meet up with some fellow canoeists, and he joined us on the river for most of the morning.

The portage (225 meters) avoiding Island Rapids, a double ledge, headed directly out from John's campsite on a rough dirt road, veering to the left until it met up with the gravel logging road, and then headed back down to the river on the right, just before a wooden bridge.

We then walked over another portage marked almost immediately on the left bank. Our government map had the trail measured at 595 meters. But like the previous portages, it felt much longer. (I paced this one at 700 meters.)

The put-in had a great campsite, and here we met another group of canoeists. We stopped to chat and, over time, began to notice that our reasons to canoe the river were far different from theirs. It had taken them three days to cover what we had paddled in a day and a half, even though they ran most of what we walked around. They had obviously spent their time taking it easy, managing not to begin each day until 11 a.m. and ending before 3 p.m. On the other hand, Alana and I were up as early as 5 a.m. and paddled at least until 6 p.m. We spent most of our time sneaking up on wildlife and saved most of our conversations with one another for around the evening fire. It was apparent that we savored the peace and quiet while they made their trip more of a social thing.

I made the contrast between our different styles of paddling with an open mind, of course. I try not to react the way most canoeists do when meeting another group on a remote river — comparing paddling traits and assuming that one's own way is the better way to travel.

We all stayed together as a group up until the next portage. The rapid here, nicknamed the Temple of Doom, has a good number of jagged rocks piled up at its base, and Alana, John and I made the cautious decision to use the 270-meter portage marked on the left bank. The others, however, were equipped with rental boats and chose to pick their way through the gigantic boulder garden.

Amazingly enough, they all made it down without any major mishaps and pushed on ahead of us to another section of rapids an hour-and-a-half's paddle downstream. Two sections of whitewater must be avoided here before you reach Shewabik Lake. Both have short portages (35 meters and 45 meters, marked on the right) but they could also be easily lined down. But again, John, Alana and I had to portage. First, because the other group had wedged their canoes on the rocks of the initial drop and blocked our way, and second, because the group had flipped their canoes over a small chute at the base of the second run and once again blocked the way. Who would have thought there would have been such a traffic jam on a remote river like the Chapleau?

By the time we reached Shewabik Lake we had each gone our separate ways. John, with his Mad River closed-deck canoe (designed by Verlen Kruger), sped across the lake in no time, and he camped on a glorious sand spit three-quarters of the way along. The other canoeists ended their day much earlier and chose a site directly across from a fishing lodge on the west shore (they ended up having to deal with a black bear that came in to feed on fish guts dropped off by the lodge owner). And Alana and I continued on, planning to end our day beyond Shewabik Lake.

By 4 p.m. we had reached the falls on the north end of Shewabik Lake. We began the portage marked to the right. It was a short carry (125 meters) but was also one of the most difficult portages en route. Not only was it uncomfortably close to the drop itself, but the put-in and take-out points were incredibly steep. Alana and I had our work cut out for us as we hauled all our gear up and over the almost perpendicular slope.

Soon after the falls, once we had checked out a collection of very faint Native pictographs (a star shape, circle and animal figures) painted on an overhanging rock-face along the south shoreline, Alana and I pulled up on a marked campsite. The site was a disaster, though, with more trash and toilet-paper mounds than the place we had stayed on the night before. Obviously the garbage was left by the same group of canoeists, who were most likely traveling a day or two ahead of us.

We moved on, carried over another portage (90 meters and marked on the right) and then, totally exhausted, ended our day by erecting our tent directly at the put-in, just minutes before a major thunderstorm moved in.

The rain continued throughout the night, and just before dawn, having had enough of Bailey trying to dig under our sleeping bags every time she heard the sky rumble above us, Alana and I rolled up the tent. We spent the morning cooking breakfast under the rain tarp.

What a godsend that tarp was. It was a perfect setup, placed back in the woods far enough to protect us from the cold wind but close enough to the river to give an excellent view while we enjoyed a second cup of camp coffee. I had tied one corner lower than the others to allow the rain water to run off in a steady stream and not collect in the middle and cause the tarp to sag.

We'd also stored dry wood underneath the night before and we had plenty of fuel to cook a big breakfast and keep the morning chill away.

A steady downpour continued throughout the morning and we even discussed calling it a rest day. The problem was that we weren't sure if we had planned enough days to complete the route so, to be on the safe side, we resigned ourselves to packing up and preparing ourselves for a soggy day out on the river.

Almost immediately down from our campsite we portaged across two consecutive 125-meter portages, the first heading across a pine-clad island, and the second marked to the right of a large chute.

The next hour of river travel was mostly with a sluggish current that flowed past giant mats of sedge grass. The only break in the monotonous paddle was exploring a side channel where a small esker split the river into two channels. The main route is to the right, but Alana and I decided to take some time out to investigate the tributary on the left. This was the route to Bonar Lake, a side trip that was used by Natives and other early explorers to avoid a long stretch of rapids downriver on the Chapleau. We saw no evidence that the portage was still being used, but our efforts were rewarded when we spotted our first moose of the trip. I was surprised that we hadn't seen a moose until now, especially since that the Chapleau River flows parallel with the Chapleau Game Reserve, established back in 1925 to help keep a healthy stock of fur bearers, and one of the largest protected areas in the world. The poor creature, however, was totally blind and so extremely vitamin-deficient that it could barely hold its head out of the water while swimming across to the opposite shore. As soon as we realized the moose was having difficulty, Alana and I paddled back to the main portion of the river, praying that nature would soon take its course and put the decrepit animal out of its misery.

Forty minutes later we approached another set of rapids. It came with a short 110-meter portage along on the right bank. By this time, however, Alana and I had become bored with carrying around every section of questionable rapids, and decided to take our chances in running it. Fortunately the heavy rains had added more water to the river and we easily shot through the center tongue.

A second set of rapids waiting for us another 30 minutes downriver wasn't as easy, though, and once again we were forced to take to the portage (180 meters and marked on the right).

At the put-in we met up with yet another group of canoeists. They had obviously chosen to spend the rainy day in camp. Upon greeting them I took notice of fresh toilet-paper mounds and a huge pile of litter dumped on their site. Alana and I had finally caught up with the guilty party — these were the people we had been cursing for the past two days. I was so infuriated with them that I kept the canoe on my shoulders and attempted to walk right past, pretending they didn't even exist. Of course, our dog, Bailey, not knowing any better, stopped for a free scratch behind the ears. One thing lead to another, and soon Alana and I were sitting down to have lunch with the hooligans.

An hour later, after sharing stories of our time spent on the river so far, my anger for these unethical canoeists hadn't changed. However, I did manage to gain a little understanding as to why they would act so disrespectfully toward nature. First, they were completely inexperienced trippers and had obviously over-packed. This, of course, forced them to lighten their load each morning before leaving camp, attempting to burn or even bury their excess food scraps, candy wrappers, bait containers, and even empty cans of beer. And second, they were absolutely terrified of their surroundings and their response was to avoid it at all costs. So, when the call came to relieve themselves, especially after dark, they would walk only a few meters away from camp to do their business.

Many canoeists, when traveling in remote areas for the first time, are similarly afflicted. The only thing that seems to cure you is experience, knowing that behind every bush can't be a bear and that cans of beer are far too heavy to pack along. It's ignorance, plain and simple. Hopefully the degenerates we met would eventually change their ways and feel more at home in the woods on their next trip. To encourage them, Alana and I gave the group a few subtle hints before leaving their camp. While Alana picked up every bit of litter around our lunch site, I wandered far back into the woods with a roll of toilet paper tucked under my arm, announcing that I was going to become one with nature.

The next couple of hours of paddling were completely miserable. The current remained sluggish and the rain continued to pour down on us. Just before the confluence of the Makonie River, things began looking up, however. Here Alana and I began running the first of five sets of continuous rapids.

This stretch of whitewater lasts for more than 3 kilometers, and even though each set has a portage marked on the right bank (180 meters, 150 meters, 90 meters, 110 meters, 315 meters), the entire section can usually be run by moderate canoeists.

Alana and I were successful on the first run, managing only to scrape a bit of paint off the bottom of the canoe. We zigzagged our way through a collection of exposed rocks on the second rapid and then came close to hitting

Alana, Bailey and I stop to visit the bustling rail town of Elsas.

the remains of a canoe that had broken apart on one of the many swifts making up the third set. The fourth and fifth rapid were the most challenging, though. Low water levels had left a shallow, sloppy mess. Deep channels were almost non-existent, especially on the last section, and we ended up wading down most of the way.

We were now completely soaked, and paddled for only another half-hour before pulling up on the take-out of another portage (270 meters and marked on the right), and then carried our gear over to make camp at the put-in.

The temperature had now dropped, changing the rain to sleet, and Alana, Bailey and I felt almost hypothermic. We shivered uncontrollably and became desperate for a fire. But igniting any flames after a daylong downpour would be a challenge to say the least. First I wrapped half a candle with strips of birch bark that I always store inside the pocket of my rain jacket, and then, in a crisscross pattern on top, I placed a handful of small dead branches collected from the base of a thick spruce tree. With quivering, wet hands I struck the match on the zipper of my camp pants, lit the wick of the candle, and then began nursing the flames with long puffs of air to dry out the wet tinder.

Soon the fire was big enough to heat up larger pieces of wood and Alana and I were even able to hang our wet clothes over a stick and roast them over the hot coals. Bailey joined us around the now roaring fire and we watched as the extreme cold air met with the warm river water, creating a shroud of mist to dance across the rapids adjacent to our campsite.

It's funny how, when at home in the city, Alana and I pay little attention to the weather. At the very most we will grab an umbrella at the front door if we notice it raining outside. Out here, however, it's a different story. Everything becomes weather dependent and we find ourselves always watching cloud formations, wind direction, or any indication that there's a drop in air pressure: an increase in bird activity, a large swarm of mosquitoes, or the way the smoke rises off the morning fire — all of which were apparent the next morning. So, knowing we soon had the expanse of Kapuskasing Lake to cross, we made a quick departure once again.

We still had to deal with the last two remaining rapids before the Chapleau River empties into Kapuskasing Lake. The first rapid, equipped with a 225-meter portage on the right, was just as shallow and rocky as the last set the day before, and we ended up wading most of it. The second run was even more of a challenge, and we ended up cracking our bow plate after coming around a blind corner and hitting a good-sized rock on the second of two main drops. (It's best to make use of the 270-meter portage on the left.)

It took longer than planned to deal with the last bit of rapids, but Alana and I still managed to reach Kapuskasing Lake at 10 a.m. As luck would have it, there was only a slight breeze coming out of the north when we passed Hemp's Camp (one of the two fishing lodges on the lake). We made a quick decision to head straight across, toward the second lodge on the lake and then to the town of Elsas, rather than play it safe and stick close to the western shoreline. It's not that we didn't have a strong reverence for such a large lake, especially one that has an average depth of only 4 meters and is well known for brewing up in high winds. But we knew that bad weather would soon be on us and there was absolutely no place to camp on the south end of the lake.

It was the wrong decision, of course. Everything seemed to be going well until we reached the halfway point. Suddenly the wind changed direction and hit us broadside. Before long, the waves had doubled in size and we grew increasingly vulnerable. At least with a headwind you can tack the canoe like a sailboat. Even with a heavy tailwind you usually have time to bail the excess water while surfing the crests of the waves. With the wind hitting us directly broadside, however, it became almost impossible to maintain control. Alana and I could only push on and hope we reached the opposite shore before the waves tripled in size.

By digging in, arms aching with the strain of each and every paddle stroke, we eventually beached the canoe at Gosenda Lodge, just in time to witness whitecaps foaming out in the center of the lake. Alana and I could see that another rainstorm was forming in the distance. In fact, a miniature rain squall had already blasted us seconds before coming to shore, so we made our visit to the fishing lodge short and hurried along to Elsas.

The small hamlet was difficult to locate at first, but by heading straight for the radio tower and then making a right, toward the railway bridge, we soon caught a glimpse of the town dock (known locally as Quigley's Landing). There to greet us was Bill Walsh, the only full-time citizen of Elsas, and Ron Quigley, owner of Quigley's bed and breakfast.

Ron opened up his business here after visiting back in 1993 while working as a chef for the railway. He and his wife, Jeannie (who says that they knew so little about the business at first that they thought a screwdriver was a kind of drink), have been offering great hospitality to passing canoeists ever since.

Alana and I couldn't pass up staying for the night, even though it was only midday and we had planned to end our day at Picnic Rock (one of only two campsites available between the north end of the Nemegosenda River and Frog Lake). So while Ron carried our gear up to one of the bunkhouses, Bill showed us the whereabouts of the local tavern and bought us our first beer. It was almost to good to be true; here we were, four days out on an eight-day trip, having a cold beer inside a reconditioned tool shed decorated with every possible knickknack available (including a hat made of Budweiser cans and a singing Billy Bass).

Elsas wasn't always so vacant. The town was first established with the arrival of the Canadian National Railway in 1912. Then Continental Wood Products opened a mill site at the confluence of the two rivers in 1923. A great number of logs were floated down from Shewabik Lake on the Chapleau and from Westover Lake on the Nemegosenda, and Elsas soon became one of the largest sawmill towns in the north. But like most small villages developed alongside the railway, the boom quickly went to bust and by the late 1930s the mill was closed and the town went to ruin.

Up until 1999 the town of Elsas actually had two year-round occupants. Raymond Groulx was Bill Walsh's neighbor, until he left for a brief visit to Foleyet and suffered a heart attack. Bill told us over a second beer that Raymond, his archenemy, was considered the mayor of Elsas due to his family connections in the area. That left Bill as acting sheriff, since he had the most guns in town, and the Quigleys as the townsfolk during the summer months.

Bill was a true character of the north. He was a man who had plenty of time on his hands to sit and think and said little when approached by outsiders. It was obvious he was uncomfortable around us — I talk far too quickly and asked too many questions — but he did share a few stories of time spent on his trap lines, animal encounters, the cold winters, and canoe trips on both the Chapleau and Nemegosenda. Rivers. (His cabin was jammed full of old newspapers, magazines and books — including, believe it or not, my book *Up the Creek*.)

I was amazed at the number of canoeists Bill had seen pass through during his time here. In fact, he claimed that it was much busier before it became a provincial waterway park in 1975. (The Ministry of Natural Resources developed the park, along with Mississagi and Lady-Evelyn Waterway Parks, in response to pressure from recreational canoeists wanting "accessible wilderness.") Canoeists would use Elsas as a gateway, not only to the Chapleau or Nemegosenda Rivers, but also to the neighboring Kapuskasing and Groundhog Rivers. Bill even recalled as far back as 1937, when Bull Hemphill, the first park ranger in the area, had to develop a campground for canoeists on the beach adjacent to the railway bridge.

Bill and his dog, Teddy, who had fallen in love with Bailey, remained with us up until he noticed a large group of canoeists landing on the town dock. They were the same paddlers we had met the day before and they were looking for lodging before taking the train out to Foleyet the next morning. True to character, Bill took one look at them, made the comment, "Some got their heads screwed on right, and some don't," and then made haste back to his crude shack situated alongside the rail line.

Ron had us up at 7 a.m. for breakfast, and while we filled up on bacon and eggs he and Bill drove our gear down to the town dock. By 8 a.m. we were on our way again. All three of us had a difficult time leaving Elsas and returning to life back on the river. Bailey missed her boyfriend, Teddy, and Alana and I already longed for the comforts of the local tavern. At least it was a great day for paddling, and by using a shortcut (a manmade channel located approximately 500 meters past the railway bridge) we reached the top end of Nemegosenda River by midmorning. It was here we met up with the solo canoeist, John Mitchell, again. He hadn't bothered stopping at Elsas the night before, thinking it was a ghost town, and we teased him mercilessly about missing the pleasures of Quigley's bed and breakfast. I'm not sure he totally believed our stories of replacing our regular freeze-dried rations with barbecued roast chicken and apple pie — but he did after he witnessed Ron, along with his daughter Rebecca and family friend Mrs. Cook, pull their motorboat up on our lunch spot later that day on Pine Lake to deliver us sandwiches and a cold beer.

John then joined us for the rest of the day, probably hoping that the Quigleys would make an evening delivery as well, and we shared an unmarked campsite about 2 kilometers before the portage leading into Frog Lake.

The site, a perfect outcrop of rock surrounded by pine and spruce, happened to be my favorite spot on the entire trip. I even preferred the Nemegosenda River itself to the Chapleau. Even though we were traveling upstream through a broad floodplain rather than being flushed down wild rapids, the Nemegosenda was a more diverse river and we happened to enjoy a lot more wildlife sightings. On our first day alone we spotted five otters, three ospreys, two bald eagles, and countless beaver, muskrat, and a wide assortment of ducks.

The only real negative aspect was the number of anglers we came across. Our first encounter was early the next morning while we took the 125-meter portage around to the right of Twenty Foot Falls. A lodge was situated here, and both the take-out and put-in were cluttered with aluminum boats. There was even a large sign that read: These cabins are not for canoeists. The anglers staying at the camp were nice enough, though, and even warned us to keep to the right channel when approaching Frog Lake. Of course, we still managed to go left somehow and found ourselves lost for a good twenty minutes.

Frog Lake was quite scenic but the designated campsite, located on the same point that holds the remains of a cabin that once housed a Native family stricken by influenza in the 1930s, wasn't as good as the unmarked site we chose before the falls.

Halfway across Frog Lake we then paddled into the southeast bay to reach the base of six sequential rapids. The first two (225 meters and 110 meters) were portaged on the left. They were easy trails, but both take-out points were located in a strong current and we had to paddle hard upstream for a few meters to reach them. We then lined the third and fourth rapid. It would have been easier to make use of the portages (45 meters on the right and 90 meters on the left), but we somehow passed by both of them while working our way up the river.

We did, however, portage around the last two remaining rapids. The first was a long 360-meter trail along the right bank, which managed to head directly across a gigantic mud puddle about a quarter the way along. The second portage, though, was just an easy extension of the first and added on only another 50 meters to avoid a small swift.

Navigating around all six rapids took us much longer than originally planned, and it was quite late, already 7:30 p.m., before we reached the next

Twenty Foot Falls on the Nemegosenda River.

possible campsite on the river. That was just before Alcorn Lake. And there, holding the spot for us, was our friend John. He had decided that afternoon, after accidentally dumping in the last set of rapids, to wait for us to catch up to him and then ask if he could join us the rest of the way. You see, this wasn't his first mishap of the trip. On the Chapleau he had also flipped out of his boat and managed to cut his leg badly. He then embedded a stick into his foot while on a portage and also had to deal with a nuisance bear while camping on Shewabik Lake. And no, he was not out of his league paddling alone out here. John had actually traveled without injury on far more remote rivers. Alana and I figured that he just felt jinxed this time around and thought it best to tag along with us to play it safe.

A thick cloud of mosquitoes buzzing outside our tent the next morning indicated more foul weather was on its way. And once again we had to contend with crossing a large body of water — Nemegosenda Lake — and had to head out early.

The rain had begun by the time we reached the south end of Alcorn Lake, and our moods seemed to match the landscape we were passing through.

The banks, once lined with stout red pine, were now scarred by wildfire, and the constant twisting of the river from here to Nemegosenda Lake made for an incredibly monotonous paddle. When we eventually did reach the lake, which marks the end of the provincial waterway park, we were glad to see that the surface was still calm enough for a safe crossing. And even though we kept close to the left shoreline — learning from our misadventure out on Kapuskasing Lake — the lull remained for the entire two hours it took us to reach the far southern bay.

Here, after lifting over a large beaver dam, we began the worst portage en route: a 1,000-meter bush trail that had at least a dozen logs strewn across it, boot-sucking mud that felt more like quicksand, and a heavy growth of saplings that completely hid the path most of the time. To make matters worse, the rain continued to pour down, and once again Alana, Bailey and I felt hypothermic.

Our original plan was to find our way up Borden River (a shallow but scenic waterway lined with cedar) and then make camp on the tip of an esker that splits the north end of Mate Lake into two distinct bays. But our truck was parked on the south end of Waweya Lake, only one portage away from Mate Lake, and we made the quick decision to go for it. So after saying our goodbyes to John, who had planned to loop back to the town of Chapleau during the next couple of days, we headed straight up an incredibly steep 450-meter path leading to Waweya Lake, making this the second-most difficult portage of the trip.

It was an exhausting way to finish an already tough day, but the late-evening paddle across the shimmering turquoise water of Waweya Lake (a nutrient-poor kettle lake formed by a chunk of melted glacial ice) was absolutely breathtaking. And after walking up a short trail to the left of the take-out of the next portage, we were happy to find our truck waiting for us.

Within half an hour, Alana and I had driven to Chapleau, booked ourselves a hotel, and ordered a large pizza. We felt a little guilty about leaving poor John back on Mate Lake to weather yet another storm. But in reply to the e-mail we sent him after our trip, John informed us that, other than having a bear give him a friendly visit, he rather enjoyed his night camped out on the esker. Besides, he was better off, in a way. Alana and I were only into our second slice of pizza when the police raided the room beside us to arrest a known fugitive. The commotion was a real shock to the system, and we realized that the comforts of civilization couldn't compare to our life back on the river.

CHAPLEAU AND NEMEGOSENDA RIVERS

TIME 8–10 days

NUMBER OF PORTAGES 35 (some can be avoided be running or lining down rapids)

LONGEST PORTAGE 1,000 meters

DIFFICULTY Intermediate whitewater and canoe-tripping skills are needed.

ALTERNATIVE ACCESS Use the public launch in the town of Chapleau, reached by Highway 101, or in the town of Elsas, which is accessible only by rail.

ALTERNATIVE ROUTE Travel the entire Chapleau-Nemegosenda route (10–12 days) by beginning and ending in the town of Chapleau. The trip can also be reduced to five days by paddling either one of the Chapleau or the Nemegosenda Rivers, beginning in the town of Chapleau and ending in Elsas. Take note, however, that you have to take a train from Elsas to the town of Foleyet and vehicles must be shuttled from the town of Chapleau or Waweya Lake, depending on which river you choose to paddle.

OUTFITTERS

MISSINAIBI HEADWATERS
Box 1207
Collingwood, Ontario
L9Y 3Y9
705-444-7780
(off season)
or
Racine Lake
Chapleau, Ontario
P0M 1K0
705-864-2065
(May to September)

QUIGLEY'S DO LITTLE INN
Kapuskasing Lake
Box 86
Foleyet, Ontario
P0M 1T0
905-825-3090

FOR MORE INFORMATION

MINISTRY OF NATURAL RESOURCES
190 Cherry St.
Chapleau, Ontario
P0M 1K0
705-864-1710

VIA RAIL CANADA
1-888-VIARAIL (1-888-842-7245)
www.viarail.ca

TOPOGRAPHIC MAPS
41 O/14, 42 B/3, 42 B/6 & 42 B/10

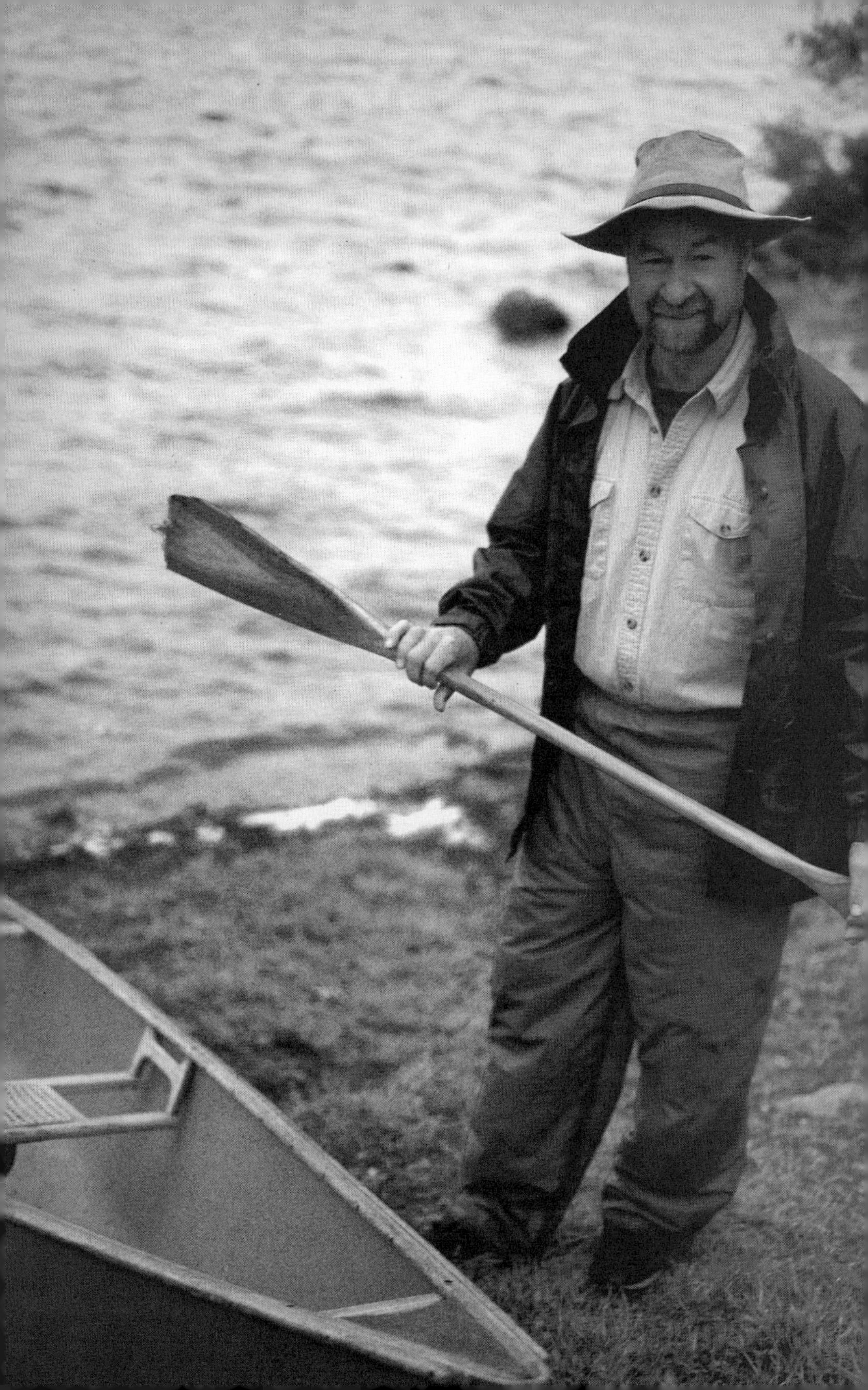

WAKAMI LAKE
LOOP

HUGH BANKS, A FELLOW INSTRUCTOR at the college I lecture at part-time, has accompanied me on a couple of obscure canoe routes in the past. So when I began working on my "lost canoe routes" project, I thought it was only fitting to ask him to tag along on at least one of the trips I had planned. My first choice was the Wakami River — a 124-kilometer unmaintained route beginning at Wakami Lake Provincial Park and ending on Howard Lake. The only problem was that in the early part of the season, the best time to run the river, Hugh had to undergo a hip replacement. And even if water levels were high enough for a possible fall trip, he still wouldn't be in shape enough to drag a boat and heavy packs through a difficult river such as the Wakami.

As luck would have it, though, Wakami Lake Provincial Park also offers a four-day circular route, perfect for novice paddlers or intermediate ones with a false hip. So on the second week in September, Hugh and I teamed up once again to head off into the unknown.

To reach Wakami, take Highway 129 and then turn east onto Highway 667, 32 kilometers south of Chapleau. The park is approximately 30 kilometers from the turnoff and located on the south side of the highway.

It was midday by the time we reached the park gate, paid for our interior camping permit, and then shoved off from the dock right next to the staff house (the safest place to store your vehicle). There was a heavy wind coming directly from the south, so it was another three hours before we managed to make camp on the far end of the lake. Obviously the translation for Wakami — "still and clear waters" — didn't apply. In seconds, massive

---

Rule number one when paddling with Hugh Banks – never let him borrow your favorite paddle.

56   ONTARIO'S LOST CANOE ROUTES

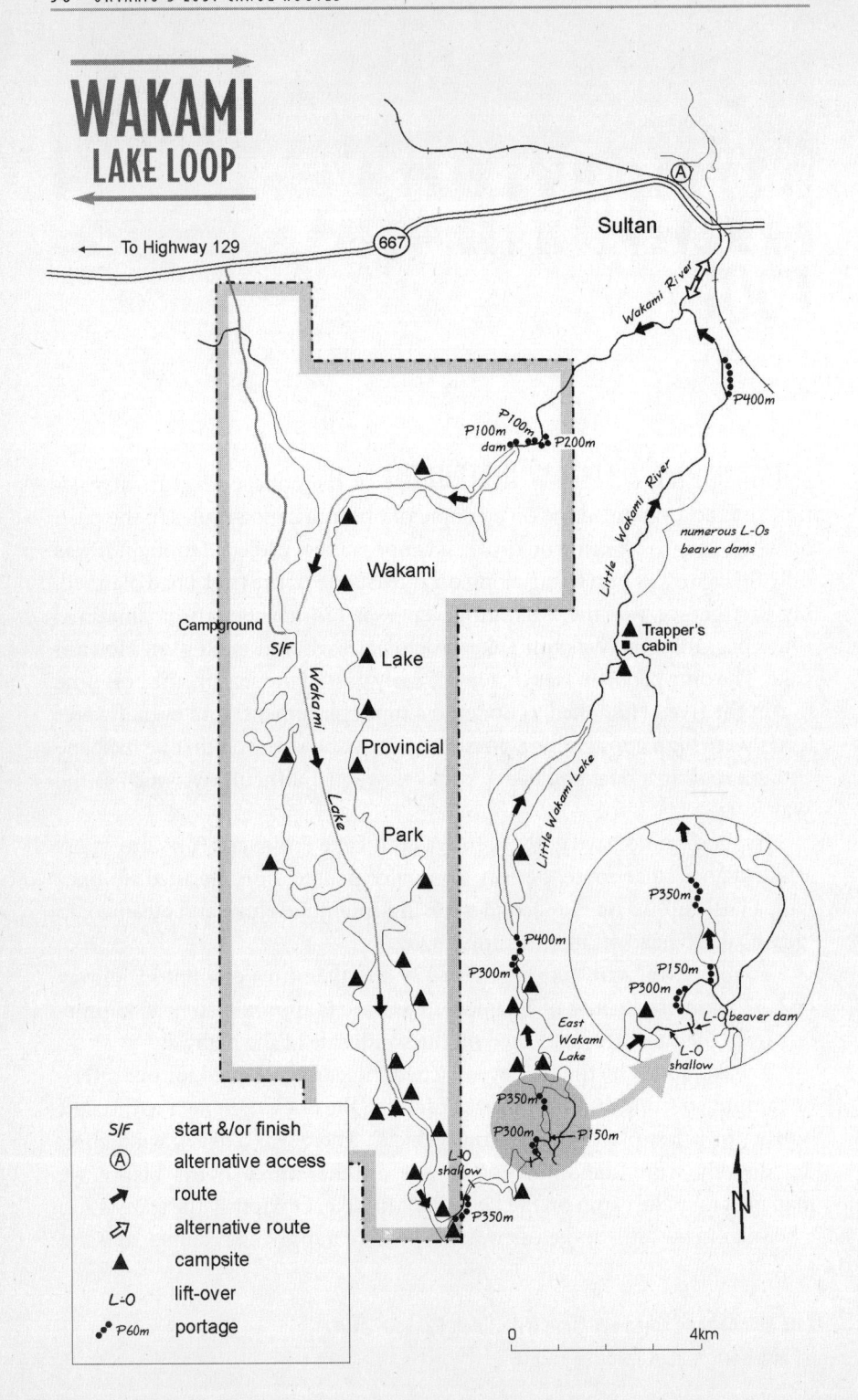

WAKAMI
LAKE LOOP

swells had built up all across the expanse of the lake, making for some very uneasy paddling. Hugh and I found our canoe dangerously close to capsizing a number of times.

Our main problem was that if we kept to the safety of the irregular shoreline it would be dark before we reached the interior campsites marked on the south end of the lake. So Hugh and I made the decision to keep paddling straight down the middle, praying the waves would remain relatively uniform in shape. It was obviously a foolish act, and every now and then a rogue wave would hit us broadside, sending a slap of cold water across the bow to remind us how vulnerable we really were out there.

Eventually, about three-quarters of the way along, we were able to give our arms a break. The lake narrowed and a protective point guarded us from the heavy winds. We even took some time out to try our luck with the local walleye population, and four fish later we continued on down the lake.

Our campsite that evening was perfect. It was situated directly at the mouth of the creek that drained into the south end of the lake, allowing us to spend the evening casting for more walleye. The site even came with its own fire grill, picnic table and well-constructed outhouse. Through the night, however, the south wind had brought in a violent storm, and come morning, Hugh and I had to really motivate ourselves to pack up and head out on the water.

In a downpour we continued south, following the creek to where the first portage of the trip (350 meters) works its way around to the right of an old sluice-box once used to transport logs into Wakami Lake. The path joins up with the park's 76-kilometer Height of Land Trail. (The trail follows Wakami's perimeter and is rated one of the most challenging in the province.) But eventually the trail crosses the creek and the portage continues on to a put-in littered with half-submerged boulders.

Low water levels made the next section difficult, and we had lost a great deal of paint from the bottom of our canoe by the time the shallow creek opened up into a small pond. However, once we reached halfway across the pond, we then continued on up a second creek. (The mouth of the creek is located just before where a prominent campsite is marked on the top of a knob of granite.)

Luckily this creek bottom was sandy, making it easy to wade up the drier parts. Also, a giant beaver dam halfway along held back enough water upstream to allow us to paddle directly to the next portage.

The 300-meter trail avoided a number of beaver dams that had made the creek completely unnavigable. It was an easy trail, though, especially since a

The water level on the Little Wakami was high, making for a leisurely morning paddle.

work crew had cleared most of the deadfall blocking the route just a week before our trip. On our return for the second load we even stopped to gorge ourselves on the clumps of blueberries growing thick under a heavy canopy of pine.

Considering the Wakami area is well known for its logging history (1928–1946), it's surprising to see how well the forest has bounced back here. Thick stands of jack pine dominate, but since the park is situated along the southern fringe of the Canadian Shield, the area is also home to sporadic patches of trees that are more common to the Great Lakes–St. Lawrence Forest region (yellow birch, sugar maple, white pine).

Everything growing here is now second growth, of course. The original forest was mostly removed by the McNaught Lumber Company. They were a subsidiary of Austin and Nicholson, who first introduced the Linn tractor — a machine that revolutionized mechanical logging in Northern Ontario and allowed McNaught to go from producing 1,000 railway ties per year to 200,000. By the time the company closed its doors, a total of 27 million board feet of red and white pine and 25 million board feet of jack pine and spruce were taken from the Wakami Lake area.

Unlike the original forest, the steep gradient the trees once grew on hasn't changed. The next portage, a 150-meter trail that's easily spotted from the previous put-in, went up and over a sharp knoll before ending in a small pond. And almost directly across the pond was another somewhat abrupt 350-meter portage, leading into East Wakami Lake.

Originally Hugh and I thought of camping on East Wakami, since park staff told us that it was the most scenic lake en route. The campsites weren't the best, though. And for a solid hour we fished without any luck. So we decided to continue on, tackling two more portages to reach Little Wakami Lake — a 300-meter trail that lead us into another small kettle lake and a 400-meter trail that had a dangerous downhill slope near the put-in.

Little Wakami Lake was less dramatic than East Wakami. It was shallow, averaging no more than 8 feet deep, and had even worse campsites to choose from. But Hugh and I managed to catch fourteen pike while we trolled across it, and half a dozen more before heading out the next morning on the Little Wakami River.

The water level on the Little Wakami River was high, making it an easy paddle. But the time spent on this constantly meandering river was absolutely exhausting. The first hour we traveled upstream to where a small creek, flushing in just east of an old trapper's cabin, marked the height of land. There were no brass bands or dancing girls to mark the separation of the Atlantic and Arctic watersheds — just a slight change in current as we passed by a bit of almost stagnant water. After that, it took another three hours to reach the Wakami River, which included lifting over half a dozen beaver dams as well as portaging 400 meters to the right of a shallow set of rapids, approximately one kilometer from the confluence.

Downstream and to the right of the river junction was the town of Sultan — a small milltown known for housing the gravesite of the vagabond poet John Ceredigion Jones, who wrote the lines now inscribed on the Peace Tower in Ottawa: "All's well for over there among his peers a happy warrior sleeps."

Hugh and I, however, went left, paddling upstream toward Wakami Lake. The river was much wider here and far less meandering. It was also shallower, forcing us to get out and wade up at least three separate sections of rapids. A couple of portages (a 200 meter on the left and 100 meter on the right) were marked on our map. But the first trail was hardly used and the second didn't exist. We even walked straight up the last section of fast water,

Remains of an old trapper's cabin at Little Wakami River.

directly below the Wakami Lake dam, lifting over on the left rather than use a 100-meter portage marked on the right.

Once on Wakami Lake, it was only another hour of paddling, first west and then south, before we would end up back at the main campground. At first we pushed hard to get there. But Hugh and I kept hooking into a pike or walleye every time we went to troll our lines out behind us. As it was getting close to dusk, we would soon have to make the decision to either reel in our lines and paddle hard to reach the comforts of the campground or stay one more night out in the interior. It was a toss-up. Dark clouds were moving in, which meant that we would have a difficult time paddling the remainder of Wakami Lake come morning. But we could also hear loud shouts, even foul language, coming from the campground.

Hugh and I finally settled on a compromise. We chose an interior site directly across from the park. It was close enough that we could safely reach it before the lake became unmanageable if there was rough weather and yet far enough away that we couldn't hear the noise made by our rambunctious neighbors. And as a bonus, we were still able to fish while taking in the wilds of Wakami Lake. Who could ask for anything more?

WAKAMI LAKE LOOP

TIME 3-4 days

NUMBER OF PORTAGES 10

LONGEST PORTAGE 400 meters

DIFFICULTY This route makes a perfect novice to intermediate trip.

ALTERNATIVE ACCESS The town of Sultan, just east of Wakami Lake Provincial Park, can also be used to link up with the loop and can be accessed by road (Highway 667) or by train (Via Rail's Bud car on the Canadian Pacific Railway).

ALTERNATIVE ROUTE Canoeists could just stay on Wakami Lake itself, enjoying a few days of fishing and even hiking a section of the Height of Land Trail that circles the lake.

OUTFITTERS

MISSINAIBI HEADWATERS
Box 1207
Collingwood, Ontario
L9Y 3Y9
705-444-7780
(off season)

or
Racine Lake
Chapleau, Ontario
P0M 1K0
705-864-2065
(May to September)

LAKE HURON CANOE OUTFITTERS
4562 Hwy. 17
Box 113
Spragge, Ontario
P0R 1K0
705-849-9043
E-mail: info@lakehuronoutfitters.com
www.lakehuronoutfitters.com

FOR MORE INFORMATION

WAKAMI LAKE PROVINCIAL PARK
Ministry of Natural Resources
190 Cherry St.
Chapleau, Ontario
P0M 1K0
705-864-1710

VIA RAIL CANADA
1-888-VIARAIL (1-888-842-7245)
www.viarail.ca

TOPOGRAPHIC MAPS

41 O/7 & 41 O/10

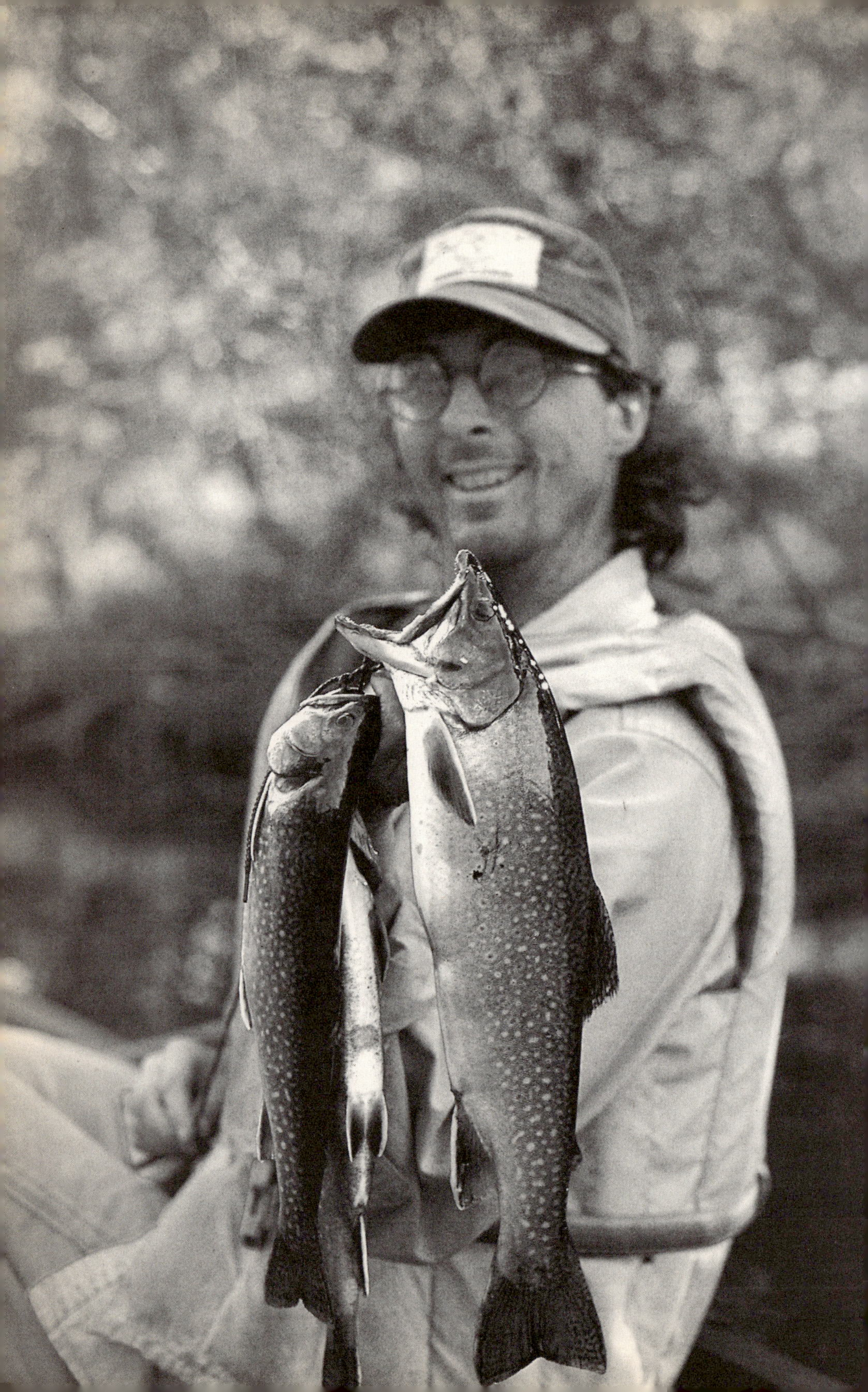

RANGER LAKE
LOOP

THE MAIN REASON I TOOK ON Algoma's Ranger Lake Loop is that it was here, at the age of twelve, that I first paddled a canoe. It wasn't an actual canoe trip. My father and I were staying at Megisan Lake Lodge — located halfway along the 104-kilometer canoe circuit — and spent a good part of the week trolling the main lake without much luck. The second-last day, my dad and I decided to borrow one of the lodge's beat-up aluminum canoes and portage into a neighboring lake to try for speckled trout. It was then that I began my love affair with the canoe. And now, twenty-five years later, it was time to return.

Things had obviously changed since then. The Ministry of Natural Resources stopped maintaining the route leading in and out of Megisan Lake in 1988. And even though Ontario Parks made the Ranger Lake Loop part of the newly designated Algoma Headwaters Provincial Park in 1999, no one in the government seemed to know much about it. In fact, my research showed that it was one of the most "lost" routes in the province. So it was only fitting that I asked the new park planners, Nancy Scott and Bob Knudsen, to tag along on my exploratory trip.

Also accompanying me were Kip Spidell and Andy Baxter. Kip and I had worked on a film together on Wabakimi Provincial Park in 1999, which happened to win the "best of" category in the Waterwalker Film Festival, and he decided that the remoteness of Algoma Headwaters would make for a perfect sequel. Andy was a friend, who somehow unknowingly volunteered to be Kip's Sherpa.

We all had wanted to paddle the entire route, beginning at Ranger Lake and then looping around by traveling upstream on the West Aubinadong

Catch of the day on the West Aubinadong River. PHOTO: SCOTT ROBERTS

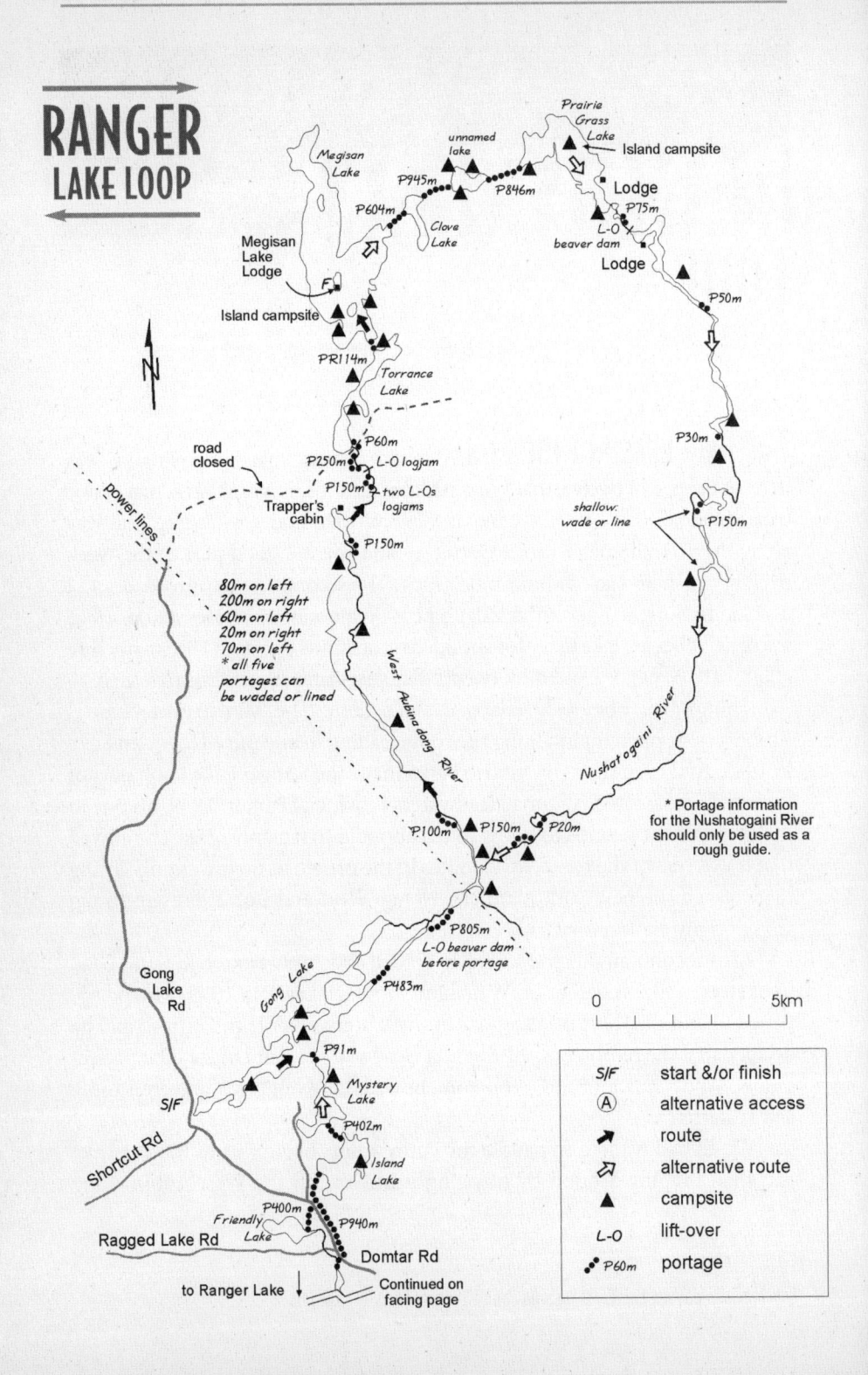

RANGER LAKE LOOP

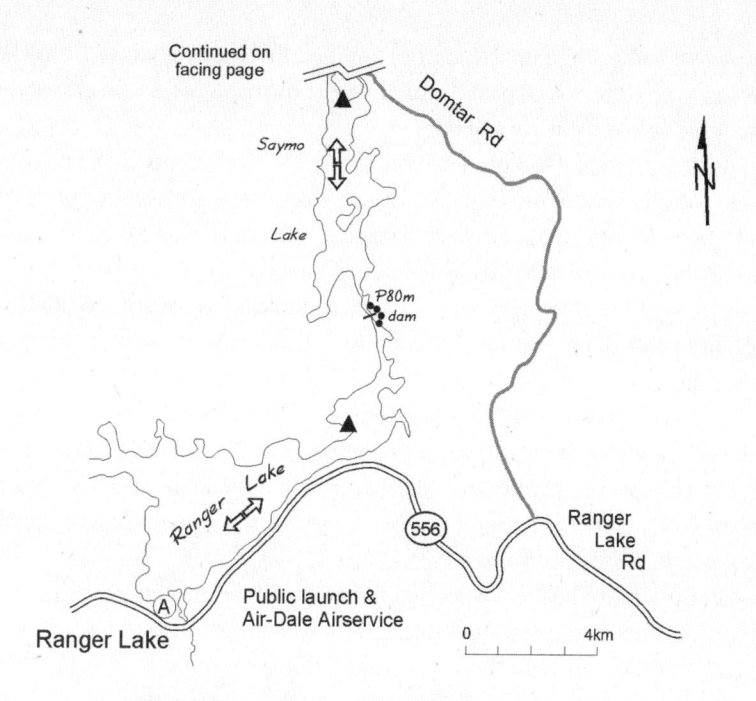

River, and then downstream on the Nushatogaini River. This would take ten days to complete, though, and we had only five. So we cheated by beginning at the Gong Lake access point — eliminating two long days of lake travel — and then omitted the Nushatogaini River altogether by being flown out of Megisan Lake and brought back to Gong. The leisurely pace would allow time for Kip, Andy and I to film, and Nancy and Bob to complete their recreational inventory. (This route would obviously be better traveled in reverse, since you would then have the current of the West Aubinadong with you.)

Andy, Kip and I, all from the Toronto area, met Nancy and Bob, both from Sault Ste. Marie, at Gong Lake (known locally as Bell Lake) at 4:30 p.m. We had planned to convene as early as 2:30 p.m. but we got a little lost along the network of logging roads on the way to the access point. The directions were simple enough — turn left off Highway 129 onto Ranger Lake Road (No. 556), drive 12 kilometers before turning right onto Domtar Road, drive another 30 kilometers along a rough road, and just past Shortcut Road turn right again on a short access road leading down to Gong Lake.

Somewhere between the bridges crossing the East and West Aubinadong Rivers we went right when we should have stayed left, and then veered left when we should have stayed right just beyond Saymo Lake. It was 8 p.m. by the time we had packed up the canoes and paddled halfway down Gong Lake to make camp. It was well past 9 a.m. the next morning when we crawled out of the tents to continue on the trip.

The first portage (483 meters) was located at the far end of the northeast bay of Gong Lake. Surprisingly, it was an easy carry, something our group didn't quite expect since we were told that the route was no longer maintained. All of us were quite delighted not to have a difficult carry first thing in the morning. Except for Kip, that is. He was looking for drama to add to his film, like a mud-filled portage littered with fallen trees and plagued by hordes of mosquitoes.

The next portage — a long 805 meters — made Kip's day, however. He soon got his wish. The trail wasn't groomed at all. Even before the take-out, we had to lift over a giant beaver dam and then choose to either bushwhack an extra 200 meters to the right of a beaver meadow or push directly through a deep patch of swamp ooze.

A couple more beaver dams had to be lifted over not far past the put-in, and Gong Creek remained shallow right up to where it passed under a hydro line and then met up with the West Aubinadong River.

Here we went left, paddling up to the confluence of the West Aubinadong and Nushatogaini Rivers. And after a quick lunch at a bush site north of the river junction, we continued up the West Aubinadong by heading left again.

We paddled 4 more kilometers upriver before calling it a day, having to deal with only a couple more beaver dams, a few shallow sections that needed to be waded, and one more brushed-over portage (100 meters and marked to the left).

Our campsite was directly across from an old clear-cut. It wasn't the best of sites, especially as it was overlooking the thin line of mature trees left behind to screen out the planted crop of monoculture jack pine.

Places like this make me wonder what's really left of our wilderness areas. In 1984, after graduating from Sault College as a forest technician, I spent two years working at both cutting trees down and replanting them. During that time, I strongly believed in the philosophy of sustainable yield — a scientific and modern approach to clear-cutting. It's something I still believe in. The problem is that somehow we managed to get ahead of ourselves. Lumber companies became greedy; technologically advanced mills increased the output but closed small milltowns; replanting same-species forests and advanced forest-fire fighting skills took away diversity; logging roads helped destroy remote areas; and, most of all, society's consumption rates continue to increase dramatically.

Old-growth pine is the big attraction at the province's newly formed Algoma Headwaters Provincial Park.

By planting over the clear-cut across from our campsite, forest managers may be able to produce lumber — all of the same vintage and size — in less than sixty years. But it will never bring back the old-growth forest that once dominated this landscape.

Even having the 44,957-hectare park protect what's left is a bit of a fallacy. In reality, it only protects the remaining old growth the way a museum protects a valuable artifact — the forest becomes an object to sit back and admire, merely helping us to recall what we once had.

Our third day out, the longest en route and certainly the most remote, helped erase negative feelings left over from camping near the old clear-cut. It took us ten hours to travel 9 kilometers. Filming the route didn't help quicken our pace, but it was actually the lack of water and a surplus of beaver dams that took up most of the day. There were also more indistinct portages to deal with. The first five (70 meters on the left, 20 meters on the right, 60 meters on the left, 200 meters on the right and 80 meters on the left), all avoiding small rapids, were clumped together where the river narrows for a 2-kilometer stretch just north of the clear-cut.

Another 150-meter portage was on the right, between two lake-like sections of the river. The trail, however, avoided only a shallow stretch that was much easier to wade up than to portage along. In fact, having become more used to walking our canoes upriver than paddling them, we had pushed our way up the entire section before noticing there was even a portage to use.

Shortly after, the river opened up again and we took time out to explore a small cabin north of the outlet. (The shack site was leased to trapper Garry Boissienau, who had recently buried his dog Barney behind the cabin and adorned the gravesite with a big white cross and a bouquet of plastic flowers.)

Another kilometer of paddling brought us to the worst set of portages yet. The first, a 150-meter trail to the left of a rock-strewn rapid, could be reached only by lifting over two logjams ahead of the take-out. The second, a 250-meter trail also found to the left, had a number of trees down across the take-out. It took us a few minutes to first locate the portage, and then a good half-hour's work with hatchets and saws to clear a path wide enough to fit the canoes and packs through.

This was a perfect time and place for an injury to occur. We were carrying over a hard-to-follow portage late in the day, with everyone beyond exhaustion. What amazed me, however, was how well we all worked together to make it through relatively unharmed. Kip did manage to twist his ankle on a tree root and Bob smacked his head quite hard on a low branch. But we all made it to the end without any serious damage.

The last portage of the day was a quick 60 meters leading into Torrance Lake. This time the take-out was clearly marked to the right. But most of the trail itself was so bushed over that we chose to lift up and over the miniature falls it avoided instead.

Windbound again on Megisan Lake.

Torrance Lake Road access, now unmaintained and soon to be removed by the ministry to control entry to this remote area, was to the left of the cascade. We thought of staying the night here — among the beer cans, fish guts and toilet-paper mounds — but decided to push on and hope for something better. It was a good call. Halfway down Torrance Lake we found a prime campsite, where inadvertently we were forced to stay for an extra night because Kip took violently ill. We never did properly diagnose him but figured it was a combination of dehydration, sunstroke and a few too many infectious mosquito bites.

The event messed up our plan to reach Prairie Grass Lake by day five. But none of us seemed to mind taking the time off. Most of the day was spent loafing around, drinking continuous pots of coffee and munching on treats. (Kip kept to herbal tea and plain white rice.) To deal with the issue of meeting Air-Dale on Prairie Grass Lake we simply had Bob call up the air service by way of satellite phone (most government workers now carry communication devices while in the interior). Now we just had to get ourselves to Megisan Lake Lodge by late afternoon the next day for pickup.

After seeing how easy it was for Bob to make contact with the outside world, the rest of the group pleaded with him to also use the phone. Everyone chose to call home. Except for me. I decided to dial up my father. Yes, I would have loved to speak with my wife. But I knew Alana would understand how special it would be to reminisce with my dad while on one of the same lakes we had paddled twenty-five years ago.

The conversation only lasted a couple of minutes before I lost my connection. Which was fine since my father isn't much of a talker. He asked how the fishing was. I answered, "Not bad," even though we'd been too busy to throw a line in yet. He asked how the weather was. I replied, "Not bad," even though it was pouring down rain and only 10 degrees Celsius (52 F) at the time. Then he wished me luck, told me to be careful, and handed the phone over to my mother.

I had mixed feelings about using the phone after that. It wasn't the short conversation I had with my father that bothered me. That's just the way he's always been. It was the idea of having a phone along on a wilderness trip in the first place. In one way, it was a great emergency device. But it also meant we hadn't really got away from it all.

Since Kip was still feeling a little nauseous the next morning, we were slow to start. And by the time we completed the 114-meter portage leading to the south end of Megisan, marked to the right of where the creek flushes into Torrance (you may consider just walking up the shallow stream rather than take the portage), strong winds had built up from the north.

Megisan Lake, the largest lake en route, was a mess. The steady gale had formed massive whitecaps that smacked hard against our hulls, and minutes later we found ourselves windbound on a miniature island in the southwest corner of the lake.

Bob unpacked the satellite phone once again to announce our change of plans to the pilot, only to discover that due to the high winds the pilot couldn't even take off from the air base anyway. So again we relaxed around camp, cooking up double helpings of lunch and dinner.

Kip and I also used the time to film. First, we walked back behind our site to record the 200-to-300-year-old white pine. Then, with a bit of artistic license, we created a make-believe scene where I ran low on food and had to resort to eating prunes and GORP (Good Old Raisins and Peanuts). Little did we know that the fictional event would soon become reality.

The wind continued to blow the next day and our pilot still couldn't take off from his home base (this was the same cold front, by the way, that formed three tornadoes that touched down in central Ontario).

Bob attempted to order in a ministry helicopter but found out the pilot had just been grounded the day before (as it happens, the same day a number of employees from the Ministry of Natural Resources were reprimanded for misusing their work computers).

We then made a run for Megisan Lake Lodge, situated on the center island. The camp was unoccupied and had limited supplies, just a few rusted cans of stew that looked as if they had been there since my father and I visited in 1978.

Bob figured the place was deserted because the previous owner, George Nixon, had just sold it to an American company. It was Nixon who first pushed for the protection of the Algoma Headwaters, claiming it was "the last virgin forest in the Sault District." In 1989, just before the province updated its Timber Management Plan, he wrote Premier David Peterson and Environment Minister Jim Bradley, asking the government to hold a special hearing for the area of Algoma District. His major concern was the cutting of old-growth pine around Megisan Lake and the construction of new logging roads that would surely allow easier access to the area.

According to an article in the *Sault Star* at the time, the Ministry of Natural Resources representative, Ron Lessard, replied that the 300-year-old pine around Megisan would likely be destroyed by fire or old age if not harvested. It would be much better to use the resource than waste it — good sound forest management. Nixon, as well as many others, including the Wildlands League, didn't agree. And now the pine are here to stay.

At 7 p.m. the winds finally died and Bob made another call to Air-Dale to arrange pickup as early as possible the next morning. The group then made themselves comfortable in the main lodge, cooking up a combination of vegetable soup mix, onion and instant potatoes (we called it Megisan Mash).

By 9 p.m. we were all bedded down. Kip and I chose the floor beside the woodstove. Nancy and Bob slept under separate dining tables to avoid being pooped on by the dozens of bats hanging from the ceiling. And Andy unrolled his foam pad directly on top of the pool table.

We awoke abruptly to the sound of a floatplane flying low overhead. Our morning pickup was an hour early, and our group had to scramble to gather up their gear before the pilot taxied up to the dock.

We then drew straws for the first flight out. Bob and I won, which was a bittersweet victory since we ended up having to change two flat tires on our vehicles while the plane returned for the second load.

It was a depressing way to end the trip, especially after already having to endure unmaintained route and then having to eat GORP and prunes for two full days. In all, though, it was well worth the hassles. Not only did I travel through some of the most scenic country the province has to offer, I had lived out a boyhood dream, and along the way reaffirmed my love affair with the canoe.

RANGER LAKE LOOP

TIME 4-5 days

NUMBER OF PORTAGES 12

LONGEST PORTAGE 805 meters

DIFFICULTY Intermediate to advanced tripping skills are required.

ALTERNATIVE ACCESS Get to Megisan Lake by floatplane or Ranger Lake by way of Ranger Lake Road (No. 556). Parking is available at Ranger Lake Lodge and Air-Dale Flying Services on Ranger Lake.

ALTERNATIVE ROUTE Paddling the route described in reverse would obviously be a better option: have Air-Dale fly you into Megisan Lake from Gong Lake or their home base on Ranger Lake. The entire Ranger Lake Loop can also be completed in 8 to 10 days from Ranger Lake or 6 to 7 days from Gong Lake. The route through Ranger Lake – Saymo Lake – Island Lake – Mystery Lake (South Anvil Lake) – Gong Lake is kept in fairly good condition by local use. The owners of the outpost camps on Megisan Lake and Prairie

Grass Lake also keep the portages between the two lakes (604 meters from Megisan Lake to Clove Lake, 945 meters to a small unnamed lake, and 846 meters out to Prairie Grass Lake) clear of major obstructions. However, the remaining route, down the Nushatogaini River from Prairie Grass to the West Aubinadong River, is quite rough. I was unable to explore this section because of unusually low water levels during the 2001 season. An old map I obtained from an area trapper does indicate a short portage and quick lift-over leading out of Prairie Grass Lake and nine portages, as well as numerous lift-overs on the Nushatogaini River itself. I've been told by some fellow canoeists who paddled the route a year before that it's no more difficult than the West Aubinadong.

OUTFITTERS

AIR-DALE FLYING SERVICES /
ONTARIO WILDERNESS
VACATIONS
Box 1194
Wawa, Ontario
P0S 1K0
705-889-2100
e-mail: ontwild@onlink.net
www.ontariowilderness.com

RANGER LAKE LODGE
Summer (May to November)
Box 175
Searchmont, Ontario
P0S 1J0
705-841-2553

EXPERIENCE NORTH ADVENTURES
488 Queen St.
Sault Ste. Marie, Ontario
P6A 1Z8
1-888-463-5957
e-mail: info@exnorth.com
www.exnorth.com

FOR MORE INFORMATION

MINISTRY OF NATURAL
RESOURCES
64 Church St.
Sault Ste. Marie, Ontario
P6A 3H3
705-949-1231

GOULAIS RIVER WATERSHED
PROJECT
736A Queen St. E.
Sault Ste. Marie, Ontario
P6A 2A9
705-256-6741

TOPOGRAPHIC MAPS

41 J/13, 41 O/3, 41 O/4, 41 O/5 &
41 O/6

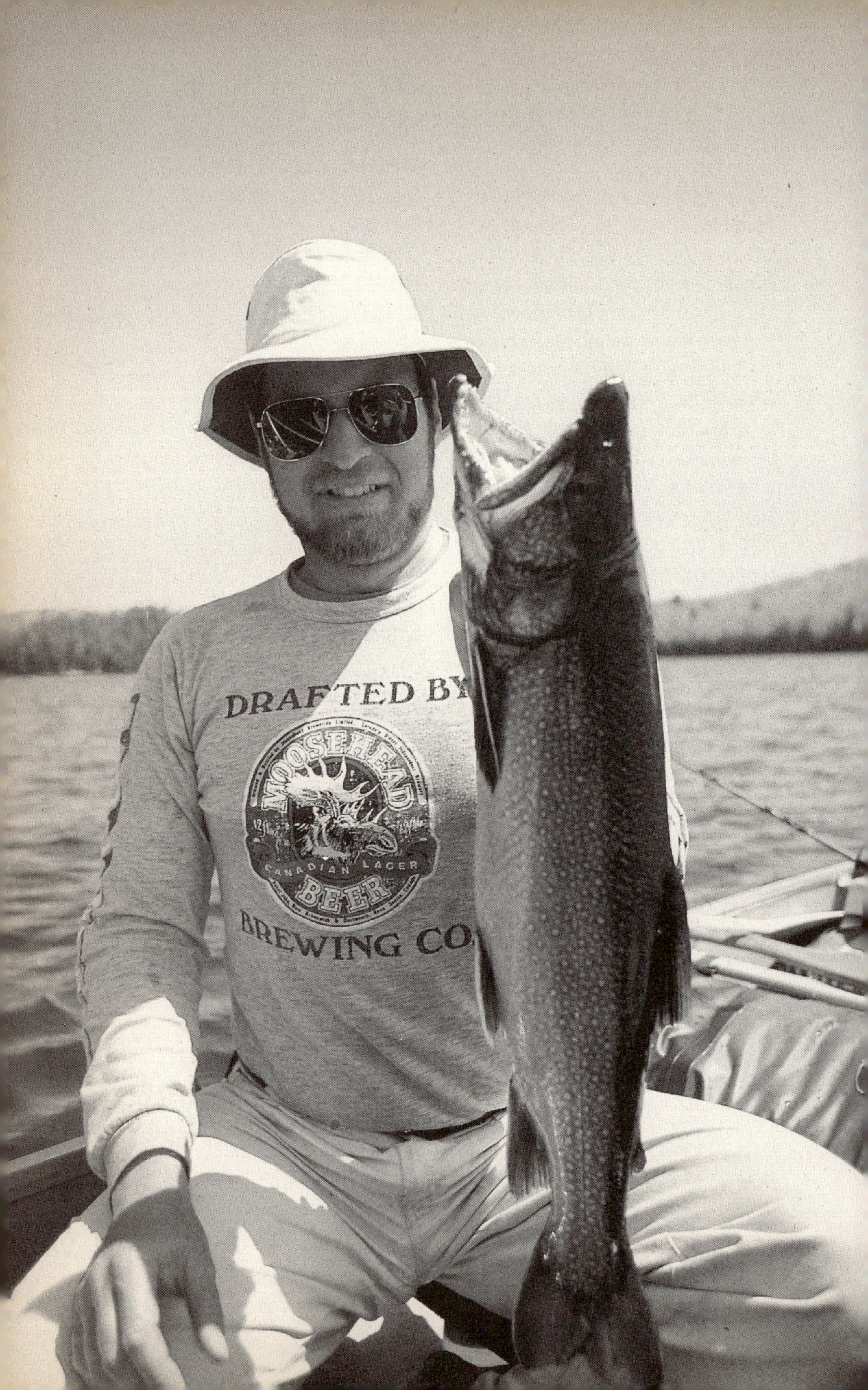
DRAFTED BY
MOOSEHEAD
CANADIAN LAGER
BEER
BREWING CO

DUNLOP LAKE LOOP

For over twelve years now a regular group of canoe mates have joined me on an annual spring fishing trip in Algonquin Provincial Park. Only once did we stray from the park boundaries, following a circuit on the Upper French River. It wasn't a bad route overall but we came back without having caught a single fish — an absolute disaster for such avid anglers as ourselves. So when I suggested this past season that we once again try somewhere new — this time a five-day loop north of Elliot Lake — they immediately rebelled.

My problem, however, was that I still had to check the route out for a magazine article that I'd promised to write. Having my regular fishing buddies along would obviously spice up the story, so I ended up having to convince them that the trip, the Dunlop Lake Loop, was far better than what Algonquin had to offer. I was lying, of course. I knew little about Elliot Lake, except that it was a mining town turned into a retirement center. But over a few beers I told them stories of short portages, uncrowded lakes, and, more important, gigantic trout just waiting to be caught. In the end, it was the falsehood of fish that convinced them to give the route a try, and come the third week in May we were, for the second time, heading north to the unknown.

Of course, upon arrival at the Dunlop Lake public launch, located on the west side of Highway 108, 10 kilometers north of Elliot Lake, the group immediately showed signs of mutiny when a local informed us that there were no fish to be had along our chosen route. He was obviously lying to us — something all good anglers do to help keep their favorite fishing hole a

Doug caught his monster splake (a hybrid between a brook and lake trout) on a two-dollar lure his son gave him at Christmas.

76 ONTARIO'S LOST CANOE ROUTES

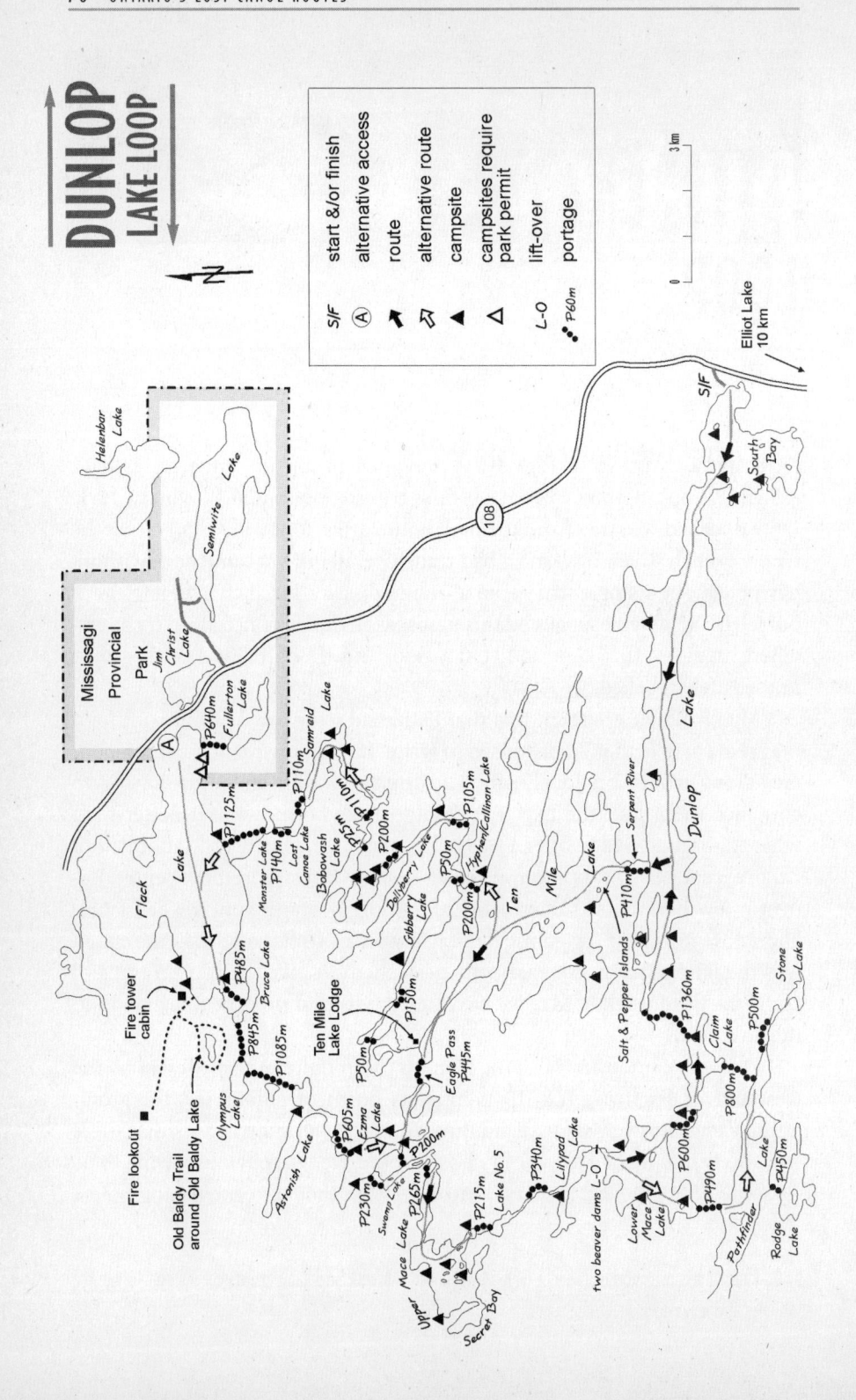

secret — but his statement did little to help my credibility. It also didn't help matters that by the time we reached the far end of Dunlop Lake — a great expanse of water that takes a good three hours to cross — not a single fish had grabbed onto our trolling lines. Even worse, a good number of motorboats shared the lake with us, eliminating any sense of seclusion. And when we took the 410-meter portage from the northwest end of Dunlop to Ten Mile Lake, the trail, marked to the left of the Serpent River, went straight up a constant rise in elevation and then ended with a huge collection of boats stacked up directly at the put-in. We were definitely not in Algonquin Park.

Ten Mile Lake was much colder and deeper than Dunlop Lake and far more difficult to navigate in heavy winds. The exposed arms of the lake, stretching from east to west, also made it impossible to keep close to the shoreline and our group could only reach the Salt and Pepper Islands, located a few hundred meters out from the portage, before we had to abandon our plans to paddle to the far side of the lake. On the north end, a perfect campsite was located right beside where a stream tumbles into Ten Mile Lake. But instead of spending our first night beside a cascading waterfall, we had to resort to a bush site west of the islands, a chunk of rock that was nowhere big enough for all six of us.

At least Ten Mile Lake was a scenic spot on which to find ourselves windbound. The entire shoreline was edged with high, rocky outcrops. It also represents one of the healthiest lake trout fisheries in the region. Of course we didn't know this at the time. An unexpected snowstorm stopped us from fishing during the usual evening calm. And we were in such a rush the next morning to make our way across the lake before the wind picked up that we kept our poles packed away the entire time.

In fact, our fishing was put on hold for most of the morning. We first had to take on the 445-meter portage leading from the northwest arm of Ten Mile Lake to Ezma Lake. It was relatively short but was steep enough for the owners of the nearby Ten Mile Lake Lodge to nickname the trail Eagle Pass. Ezma Lake, the first of a chain of smaller lakes en route, seemed like a perfect spot to wet a line, but it was one of the few selected lakes in the newly formed Blind River Provincial Park that is closed for fishing until the Saturday of the long weekend in May. And of course, we arrived on the Friday.

The next lake was Swamp Lake. It's connected to Ezma Lake by either a 200-meter portage located on the south end of the lake or a 230-meter portage to the north, marked to the right of the outlet stream.

True to its name, Swamp Lake was far too weedy to hold any trout. So again we continued on, completing another 265-meter portage on the west side of the outlet to Upper Mace Lake. But the water here remained shallow and murky as well, making the group become extremely anxious, and it wasn't until the long eastern inlet opened up that there was enough water to actually throw out a line. Of course we all cast out together and it didn't take long for our lines to become a jumbled mess. Amazingly, however, as each of us reeled in to begin untangling the mixup, four hefty lake trout grabbed on to the assortment of lures. It was an incredible event, to say the least, especially when each fish weighed more than eight pounds. By the time we had landed them all, and then chosen one of the many perfect island campsites dotting Upper Mace Lake to enjoy a shore lunch, the group had decided to renounce their distrust toward my route choice and vote me back as trip leader once again.

We spent the rest of the afternoon fishing, of course. Doug and Peter landed two more lake trout just out from the beach along the west shore and the rest of us caught half a dozen splake (a hybrid between brook and lake trout) near the entrance to Secret Bay, on the extreme southwest end of the lake.

Already excited by its healthy fish population, we found Upper Mace Lake the most scenic spot en route. Precambrian bedrock, capped with large chunks of quartzite that were dropped here by the last glacier 10,000 years ago, surrounds the lake and creates a breathtaking backdrop for the classic stands of pine, spruce and balsam fir. I can honestly say that if the lake had proved to be completely void of fish, the group would still have enjoyed their time here.

A rugged landscape, as well as exceptional fishing, continued to impress us throughout the next day. Even the portages taking us in and out of a small pond named Lake No. 5 — a 215-meter trail beginning on the east side of Upper Mace Lake and a 340-meter trail from the south end of Lake No. 5 to Lilypad Lake — gave a clear view of how compelling the rock is in this area. Both portages cross exposed granite, following closely alongside a series of falls and rapids, and keep to an obvious fault-line created eons ago when the two-billion-year-old Precambrian Shield was uplifted and penetrated by violent volcanic eruptions.

The barren rocky uplands disappeared the moment the last portage descended into Lilypad Lake, but the weed-choked floodplain provided an excellent place to spot moose. By the time our group had reached the far east side, where we were forced out of our canoes to lift over two giant beaver dams (an old trail can also be used along the left bank), we had counted two adults and three calves.

One way to deal with the bugs.

After pushing our way through the sludge of Lilypad Lake it was nice to head out into the clear water of Lower Mace Lake. It was similar to Upper Mace but without the islands. And while paddling across to have lunch on a rock outcrop, we were also able to hook into a couple of nice lake trout. So, keeping to the trip's relaxed pace, we decided to make camp early once again and then spent the remainder of the day fishing. By nightfall the group had caught seven more lake trout on the main lake and four gigantic speckles (the largest weighing over six pounds) on one of the smaller side lakes.

Taking our time on this route was obviously paying off. So many times before, while traveling through the interior of Algonquin, we had to push ourselves to make some distance before sunset, all the time paddling over some of the best fishing holes in the park. On this trip, however, we had lost our intensity — planning five days to cover what could have been done in three — and now it was paying off considerably.

The following day was actually our longest en route. It didn't have to be. To loop back to the familiar Dunlop Lake we simply had to portage in and out of Claim Lake. (A 600-meter trail is marked on the east end of Lower Mace and a long but relatively flat 1,360-meter trail is found in the northeast bay of Claim Lake.) But our group wanted to extend the day by exploring Pathfinder Lake, which later connects up with Claim Lake from the south. Both portages (490 meters and 800 meters) that lead in and out of Pathfinder were quite overgrown and none of us hooked into a single fish. The lake itself, however, was well worth the time and effort, and we made up for our lack of angling success when we reached Claim Lake. While drifting across toward the 1,360-meter portage leading into Dunlop Lake, Doug managed to hook a trophy-size splake with his two-dollar lure given to him by his son at Christmas. To add to the excitement, Kevin, the newest member of our crew, noticed a large male bear pacing back and forth at the take-out for the portage. At first we gave Doug's catch far more attention than the bear. But after the giant splake was reeled in and released we noticed that the bear was still hanging around and we began to feel uneasy. We grew even more concerned when the closer we got to the portage, the more complacent the bear seemed to become. Only when we smacked our paddles hard against the gunwales of the canoes did he actually begin to wander slowly back into the woods.

We were close to panic at this point and decided the only safe way to take on the portage was to stay close together and complete it in a single carry. It seemed foolish, but even if the bear didn't stalk us he would surely ransack anything we left behind for the second load.

Mike Walker and Doug Galloway have been canoe partners for over twelve years and have miraculously continued a strong friendship throughout it all (Bobowash Lake).

Huddled close together we stumbled our way down the path, ridiculously over-burdened with packs and canoes. The forest grew thick alongside the trail and at every bend we imagined the bear standing there, waiting to attack. Our nervous energy got us to at least halfway before the length of the portage and the heavy loads forced us to stop for a break. Of course, that's when Kevin announced a washroom break was in order. His canoe partner, Dave, pleaded with him to keep moving but he informed us that this would be his first bowel movement of the trip and that he simply couldn't hold it. So Kevin wandered off the trail, taking only a few steps away from us, and then asked us to stand guard as he relieved himself. That's when I realized how paranoid we'd become and, being the practical joker of the group, I screamed out "bear!" It was absolutely hysterical, though I admit it was cruel, to watch poor Kevin run the trail with his trousers down to his knees.

Exhausted and immensely relieved, we reached the end of the portage thirty minutes later without a single bear encounter and began our long paddle across Dunlop Lake. We figured if we made it most of the way across the 13-kilometer lake at the end of day four, we could use the morning calm

Doug hooks into another trophy trout on Claim Lake.

of day five to quickly paddle to the launch site along the west side of Highway 108, leaving us plenty of time for the long drive home.

It was 6:30 p.m. by the time we stopped at one of three island campsites three-quarters of the way across. During the long paddle, however, Doug managed to catch three more lake trout on his no-name lure and we were able to dine on fish fillets on our last night out. We left Peter in charge of cooking up the fish. There's no better person in our group to fry up trout. He insists on a fire rather than a cookstove, and, over the bed of hot coals, he heats up a gigantic cast-iron skillet, a heavy thing that's foolishly carried over each and every portage.

Usually we spend the last evening cooking up various homemade freeze-dried recipes, and the worst meal is the deciding factor of who washes the dishes. But we had enough fresh trout to feed everyone in the group that night and we changed the dish-washing rule to whoever caught the smallest fish of the trip. My canoe partner, Scott Roberts, was the winner with a three-pound speckle. Not bad, since he caught the largest fish the previous year in Algonquin, and it weighed a mere two pounds. But rules are rules. Plans are already in the works for a return trip to Elliot Lake next spring so poor Scott can redeem himself.

DUNLOP LAKE LOOP

TIME 3-5 days

NUMBER OF PORTAGES 8

LONGEST PORTAGE 1,360 meters

DIFFICULTY This is a perfect novice to intermediate route.

ALTERNATIVE ACCESS Dunlop Lodge, situated at the end of Dunlop Lake Road, may be a safer place to store your vehicle than the public launch (the lodge asks for a moderate fee for both parking and lake access). Use the Flack Lake launch, located further north along Highway 639, if you wish to paddle the extended loop. Take note, however, that you must obtain a parking permit from Mississagi Provincial Park.

ALTERNATIVE ROUTE The Flack Lake circuit route can be paddled on its own or used to extend the Dunlop Lake loop by two to three days. The Flack Lake Loop consists of Bruce Lake - Olympus Lake - Astonish Lake (the best lake overall) - Ezma Lake - Ten Mile Lake - Hyphen Lake - Callinan Lake - Dollyberry Lake - Bobowash Lake (my second favorite en route) - Samreid Lake - Lost Canoe Lake - Monster Lake - and back to Flack Lake. In general, the portages are steeper and the fishing is not as good as on the Dunlop Loop. However, the rugged scenery is far more appealing.

OUTFITTERS

LAKE HURON CANOE OUTFITTERS
4562 Hwy. 17
Box 113
Spragge, Ontario
P0R 1K0
705-849-9043
E-mail: info@lakehuronoutfitters.com
www.lakehuronoutfitters.com

FOR MORE INFORMATION

MISSISSAGI PROVINCIAL PARK
Box 37
Massey, Ontario
P0P 1P0
705-848-2806 (June to September)
705-865-2021 (October to May)

TOPOGRAPHIC MAPS

41 J/9 & 41 J/16

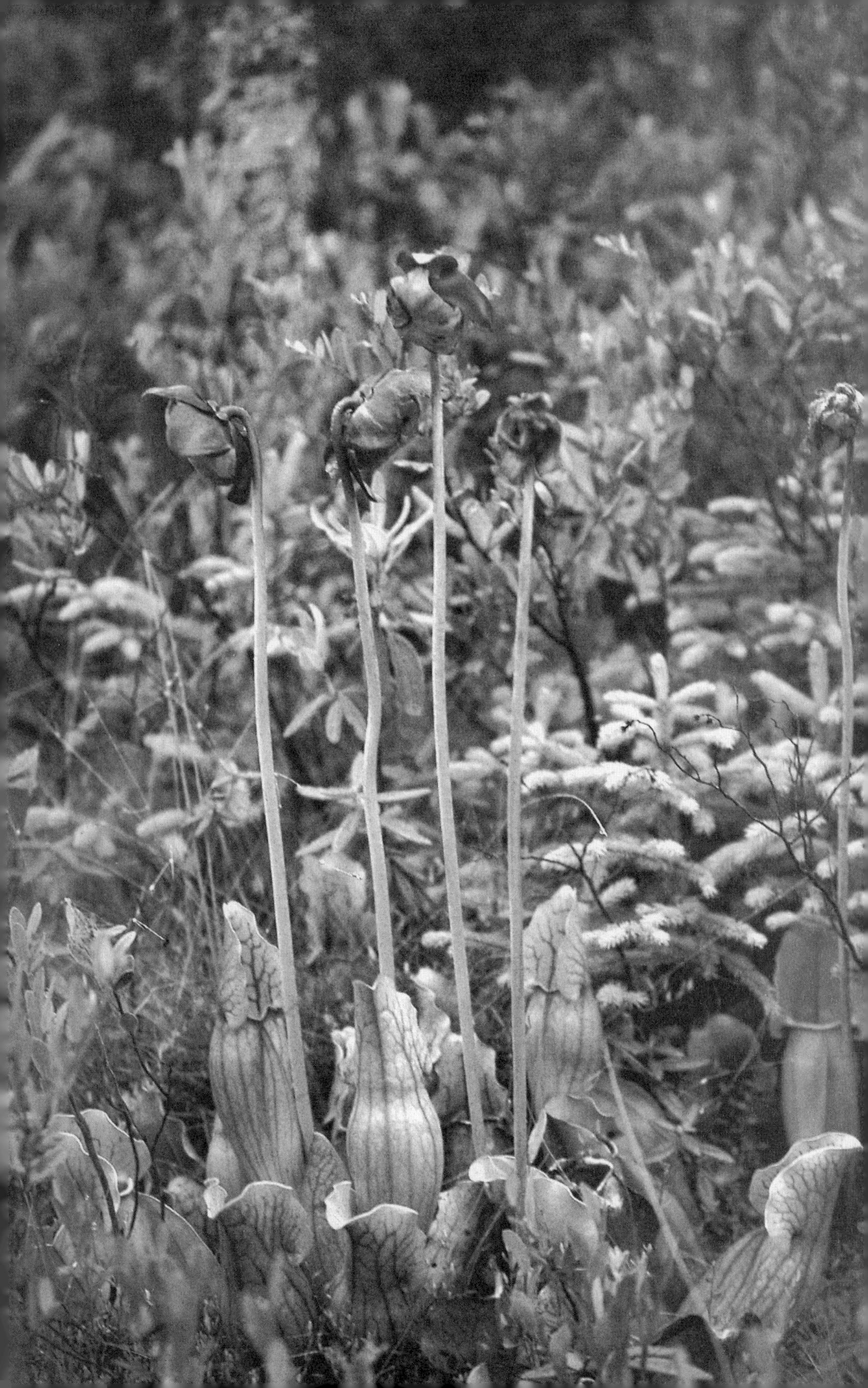

LAC AUX SABLES
BARK LAKE LOOP

MY WIFE AND I FIRST VIEWED BARK LAKE while paddling down the Mississagi River in 1996. It was a quick glimpse. We paddled across the extreme north end while visiting the cabin once used by Archie Belaney — later known as Grey Owl. But it was enough to make us want to return and explore all that we had missed before. However, rather than revisit the 177-kilometer river route, which required an extremely costly car shuttle and at least eight days of paddling, Alana and I decided to try a shortcut — a little-known circle route, accessed from Lac aux Sables, south of Bark Lake.

The launch area is located 83 kilometers north of the town of Massey, just beyond where Highway 553 and the 810 ends. It's a rough ride most of the way, with the worst section being the last 7 kilometers, past Ritchie Falls Resort. And since both Alana and our canoe dog, Bailey, suffered numerous bouts of carsickness on the way in, it was quite late by the time we pushed off from the access point.

Our tardy departure ended up being a positive thing. Originally we had planned to paddle the full length of Lac aux Sables and then make camp on the first possible campsite along the River aux Sables. However, by 5 p.m. we found ourselves only at the entrance to the northwest bay of the lake, still a couple of kilometers away from the river mouth, and decided to make camp on a small rock outcrop.

Seconds after setting up the tent, a massive thunderstorm struck, probably brought on by the intense heat of the day. With it came large hail and turbulent winds, strong enough to snap two of the four nylon ropes holding down our tarp. It was a frightening experience, especially for poor Bailey, who

Pitcher plants take root along the portage between Mud Lake and Mud Dog Lake.

86 ONTARIO'S LOST CANOE ROUTES

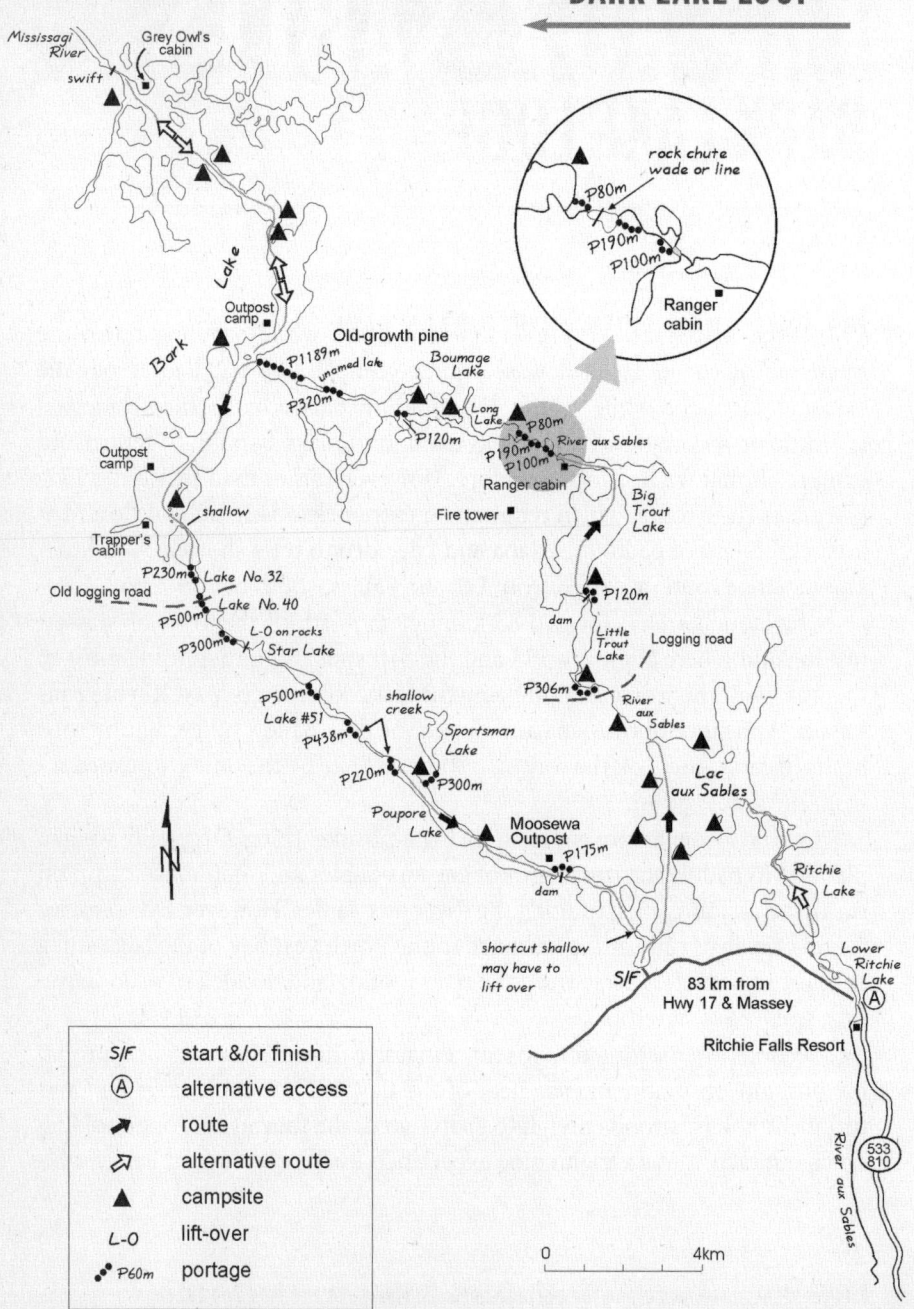

has a terrible phobia of such extreme weather disturbances. It wasn't until Alana and I began paddling up the river the next morning, however, that we realized the brunt of the storm had actually missed us. A kilometer or so upstream a wind-burst had toppled over a couple-dozen trees, with the worst area affected being the campsite we had initially planned on occupying. (The toilet seat from the outhouse had actually been catapulted across the river.)

On a positive note, the heavy rains did manage to raise the water level enough to keep our feet dry for the first few kilometers upriver. It wasn't until just before the place where a new logging road crossed River aux Sables that we had to finally get out and wade.

Not far past the bridge we also had to portage. However, the 306-meter trail, found to the left of a former log sluice, was an easy walk — especially since most of its length was along a well-maintained ATV trail.

Not long after the portage, where the river turns sharply to the right, we entered Little Trout Lake and then, eventually, Big Trout Lake by way of a 120-meter portage to the right of an old dam.

Both lakes are incredibly scenic, with a mixture of sand beaches and rock outcrops making up most of the shoreline. We held off choosing a lunch spot, though, until we linked back up with River aux Sables. The entrance, located at the far northwestern inlet of Big Trout Lake, is to the right of an abandoned shack, once used during the 1950s by forest rangers operating the neighboring fire-tower.

Wading was necessary almost immediately once we were back on the river, and this section proved far more challenging than the lower half. The gravel base had now been replaced by mud, lined with marsh grass and teeming with leeches.

Portaging also became an ordeal. The first trail — a faint 100-meter path to the left of a large beaver dam — was the easiest. Surprisingly, though, it wasn't even marked on our route map. The second portage was much more tedious. It was a short distance (190 meters) and the path itself was an easy walk. But finding the take-out was a real problem. We eventually found it to the extreme left of where the river flushes into a shallow marsh, marked only by a rusty beer can mounted on a stick. Finding the third portage — an 80-meter trail leading directly into Long Lake — was less of an issue. The dilemma here was that Alana and I had to push the canoe through an almost stagnant pond and then wade waist-deep up a rock-lined chute before actually reaching the trailhead.

After dealing with the obstacles on River aux Sables, Alana and I chose to take on only one more portage — a 120-meter trail that connects Long Lake and Boumage Lake — before making camp. Once on Boumage, however, a small forest fire burning on the east shore forced us to change our plans. The fire was probably brought on by the hot weather. Or maybe even ignited by a lightning strike the night before. Whichever the reason, we knew it wasn't wise to camp there. To play it safe we chose to continue on, all the way to Bark Lake. It was a much larger body of water and even had a couple of outposts camps equipped with radiophones if the fire happened to get out of hand.

Of course, that meant we had two more portages to endure. The first, located at the end of Boumage Lake's western inlet and leading into a small, unnamed lake, wasn't too bad. Both the put-in and take-out had a soggy bog to wade through. But the distance was only 320 meters. The second portage, however, was a long 1,189 meters. And to make matters worse, the recent storm had also forced trees down across the trail. And these weren't ordinary trees — they were massive, 300-year-old pine.

The pine, left over from the historic 1948 Mississagi fire, which burned over half a million hectares of forest, represented one of the most impressive stands of old growth in the province. They also presented a major obstacle for Alana and me. It was a stressful time, to say the least, trudging through a tinder-dry forest, knowing a small fire was burning only a few kilometers away.

It wasn't until we caught a glimpse of a government spotter plane flying low overhead, followed soon after by a Ministry of Natural Resources helicopter, that we eased up a bit. In retrospect, apart from climbing up and over a few giant pine, wading through a mud-filled bog near the take-out and then getting lost for a few minutes at a fork in the trail (make sure to go right where the portage splits closer to the put-in), pushing ourselves all the way to Bark Lake was well worth the effort. Alana and I found a spectacular beach site 2 kilometers north of the portage and, since we were now ahead of schedule, made the decision to spend two full nights here.

We awoke in good humor, knowing all we had to do on day three was paddle a couple of hours further north on Bark Lake to pay homage to Grey Owl's cabin. The site, situated directly where the Mississagi River flushes out of the northwest end of Bark Lake, had changed little since our time here five years before. The cluster of buildings was still privately owned and had just received a fresh coat of paint. The main log structure, noted for housing Archie Belaney (Grey Owl) and senior ranger William Draper in 1914, as well as the painter Tom Thomson and friend W. S. Broadhead on a two-month sketching trip in 1912, was also in relatively good condition.

I was quite surprised that it was still standing. The main cabin was built in 1908 to serve as a base for the Mississagi Forest Reserve (and also later used as

Bailey tries to snag a breeze to keep the bugs away (Bark Lake).

a Junior Ranger Camp before being sold off in the late 1970s). But the wood used was even older. The Forestry Department made use of the lumber left over from the Hudson Bay post that was abandoned on Upper Green Lake in 1892.

Revisiting the historical site was definitely a highlight. But what really made the day was our leisurely paddle back. We stopped for lunch and a swim on one of the many islands scattered across the top end of the lake, and then spent the rest of the afternoon fishing for monster pike along the heavily timbered shoreline. We even spent some time chatting with a local trapper and his wife who were out trolling for lake trout.

The couple was amazed at how well my wife and I paddled together. I guess it's true that matching up with a perfect canoe partner is next to impossible. And it's especially true that spouses usually don't mix well in a boat. But I had to agree that Alana and I were a good team while out on a trip. It's not perfect, mind you. There have been times in mid-rapid when I've yelled left and Alana went right, and yes, I've disappeared to collect more firewood just as camp dishes were about to be washed. But for the most part we communicate well in stressful circumstances and share camp duties equally.

Of course, to realize how well our relationship in a canoe works, we've both had to endure one or two disastrous trips with other less compatible partners. As a rule we've now learned not to share a canoe with those whose most important item is their beer supply. We also stay clear from individuals who have a tendency to discuss only religion and politics around the evening fire, or, even worse, constantly brag about how fit they are but continue to choose to carry the lightest load across the portage.

The trapper and his wife also seemed a well-suited pair. They were both from the Toronto area but preferred to spend most of their time together out at their cabin, located at the far south end of Bark Lake. They knew the area well, except for the route Alana and I had planned on taking back to Lac aux Sables — which seemed odd, since it began not far from their cabin.

Feeling a little uneasy about what lay ahead of us, Alana and I were packed up by 6 a.m. the next morning. By 8 a.m. we had reached the far end of Bark Lake, keeping to the left-hand shoreline all the way until a narrow inlet led us into the most southerly bay.

On the way down the lake, the landscape seemed less dramatic. The large pine were replaced by second growth, and some sections of forest had been recently clear-cut. Wildlife sighting still remained good, however. We spotted an osprey, a golden eagle and a nesting pair of bald eagles sharing the same thermal of hot air and counted fourteen loons gathered between a large island and the southern inlet.

The paddle across Bark Lake went smoothly, especially considering it is such a large piece of water. And it wasn't until Alana and I turned left at the end of a cluster of islands, entering a weedy bay to begin searching for the first portage, that we felt anxious again about our chosen way back to Lac aux Sables. There was no doubt that the route had been used before, maybe even recently. But we had little to go on. No trip notes or updated government maps existed for this section. And the tension built up until Alana took note of another beer can mounted on a stick, approximately 30 meters to the right of where a small creek entered the bay.

Once we located the concealed portage the rest was easy. The 230-meter trail went up a moderate slope and then across a floating bog to reach the north end of Lake No. 32 — an almost stagnant pond that Alana and I decided to nickname Mud Lake.

The next portage, almost directly across the pond, was easier to locate. The 500-meter trail wasn't as direct, however. Halfway along, an old logging road crossed our path. The portage started up again less than 20 meters to the left. Of course, we went right.

A small, weedy creek joins Thatcher Lake with Poupore Lake.

We eventually retraced our steps and found our way to the put-in on Lake No. 40. It was here that we almost lost poor Bailey. The dog fell into a pool of muck and then sank like a rock, weighed down by her pack full of kibble. Alana and I were too busy trying to find a way out of the swamp ooze ourselves to notice Bailey's predicament at first. We could hear her whimper. But our dog always whines on portages. It wasn't until I turned around to call her into the canoe that I noticed that only the dog's head was poking out from the slime. I had to reach down into the mud, grab her collar, and then yank her free. Lake No. 40 was then renamed Mud Dog Lake.

The next portage — a 300-meter trail that leads into Star Lake — was the most difficult en route. Locating the take-out wasn't a problem. We simply had to paddle across from the previous portage, make our way down a rock-lined creek, and then pull out on the right shore once we ran out of water. However, getting the canoe and gear unloaded and then carried across the slippery boulders just before the take-out was another story. Even after completing the portage (be sure to go right another 50 meters when the trail meets back up with the creek), we still had another stack of boulders to lift over before we could enter the main lake itself.

Star Lake is divided into two sections, making it somewhat larger than the first two ponds we had paddled across. But the water level was still as low and the quality just as poor. It did improve somewhat as we approached the next portage, located at the end of the second half of the lake, but not enough to trust filling our water bottles.

Maybe we were being somewhat phobic. After all, a local trapper, Ron Thatcher, had built his main cabin at the portage some years ago. But then again, some locals in the town of Massey had told us that Ron never did drink much water.

We easily spotted the beginning of the 500-meter trail leading into Lake No. 51 (which Alana and I were calling Thatcher Lake). There were two aluminum boats, owned by Moosewa Outpost on Poupore Lake, pulled up on shore there. But nothing much remained of Ron's cabin, just some debris stacked up in a center of a makeshift campsite. (We later found out that it had burned down three years before.)

We used the campsite as a lunch spot before moving on, and then spent the rest of the afternoon taking on a couple more portages. The first, measuring 438 meters, was to the right of where a creek empties out of Lake No. 51. (This time the take-out was marked with a beaver skull tied to a tree rather than a beer can mounted on a stick.) Then, after paddling twenty minutes down a widening in the creek, we began the second portage that led into Poupore Lake. The 220-meter trail, also marked on the right, was the best yet. Moosewa Outpost, situated at the far end of the lake, had obviously kept it clear for their moose-hunting clients. We later discovered that it was the owner, Jamie Budge, who had cleared most of the portages along our entire route. He definitely got on our Christmas card list that year.

Alana and I decided to end our day on Poupore Lake rather than camp on the familiar Lac aux Sables, linked to Poupore by an easy 175-meter portage found between Moosewa Lodge and an old dam.

Poupore was a scenic lake but lacked adequate campsites. The first place we checked out was a slab of rock on the left-hand shore, near where a bush trail leads into Sportsman Lake. The fire ring was filled with broken liquor bottles, though, so we moved on down the lake and chose a small island, using a patch of moss a little larger than a doormat to set up our tent.

It wasn't the best campsite we've ever stayed at. But it represented what we liked about the route we had just taken on, as well as all the other trips Alana and I had shared that season. Each one was set outside a manicured park, in a place where portage signs and designated campsites were definitely not the norm. It was frustrating at first, finding ourselves constantly lost and having to stop for the night at some inhospitable bush site. But by mid-summer we had grown used to it. Actually we craved it, preferring to guess our way through a grown-over portage, knowing that each one would take us deeper into the wilderness. And, when setting up camp at a place where few had stayed before, we both felt we had actually earned the right to be there.

LAC AUX SABLES: BARK LAKE LOOP

TIME 4–5 days

NUMBER OF PORTAGES 13

LONGEST PORTAGE 1,189 meters

DIFFICULTY Intermediate canoe-tripping skills are required.

ALTERNATIVE ACCESS Lower Ritchie Lake Dam, 76 kilometers north on Highway 553/810.

ALTERNATIVE ROUTE To avoid driving the last bit of rough road between Ritchie Falls Resort and Lac aux Sables, it is possible to paddle north from Lower Ritchie Lake Dam to reach Lac aux Sables. In low water it may be best to paddle to Bark Lake and back by way of River aux Sables and avoid the ponds altogether. In high water conditions it is also quite possible to paddle the entire loop clockwise, which would allow you to paddle downstream on River aux Sables.

OUTFITTERS

RITCHIE FALLS RESORT / MOOSEWA OUTPOST
Box 5259
Espanola, Ontario
P5E 1S3
Camp: 705-965-2490 (after 1 ring and tone sound, dial 036)
e-mail: jhorn@tbaytel.net
www.tbaytel.net/jhorn

LAKE HURON CANOE OUTFITTERS
4562 Hwy. 17
Box 113
Spragge, Ontario
P0R 1K0
705-849-9043
e-mail: info@lakehuronoutfitters.com
www.lakehuronoutfitters.com

TOPOGRAPHIC MAPS
41 J/9 & 41 J/16

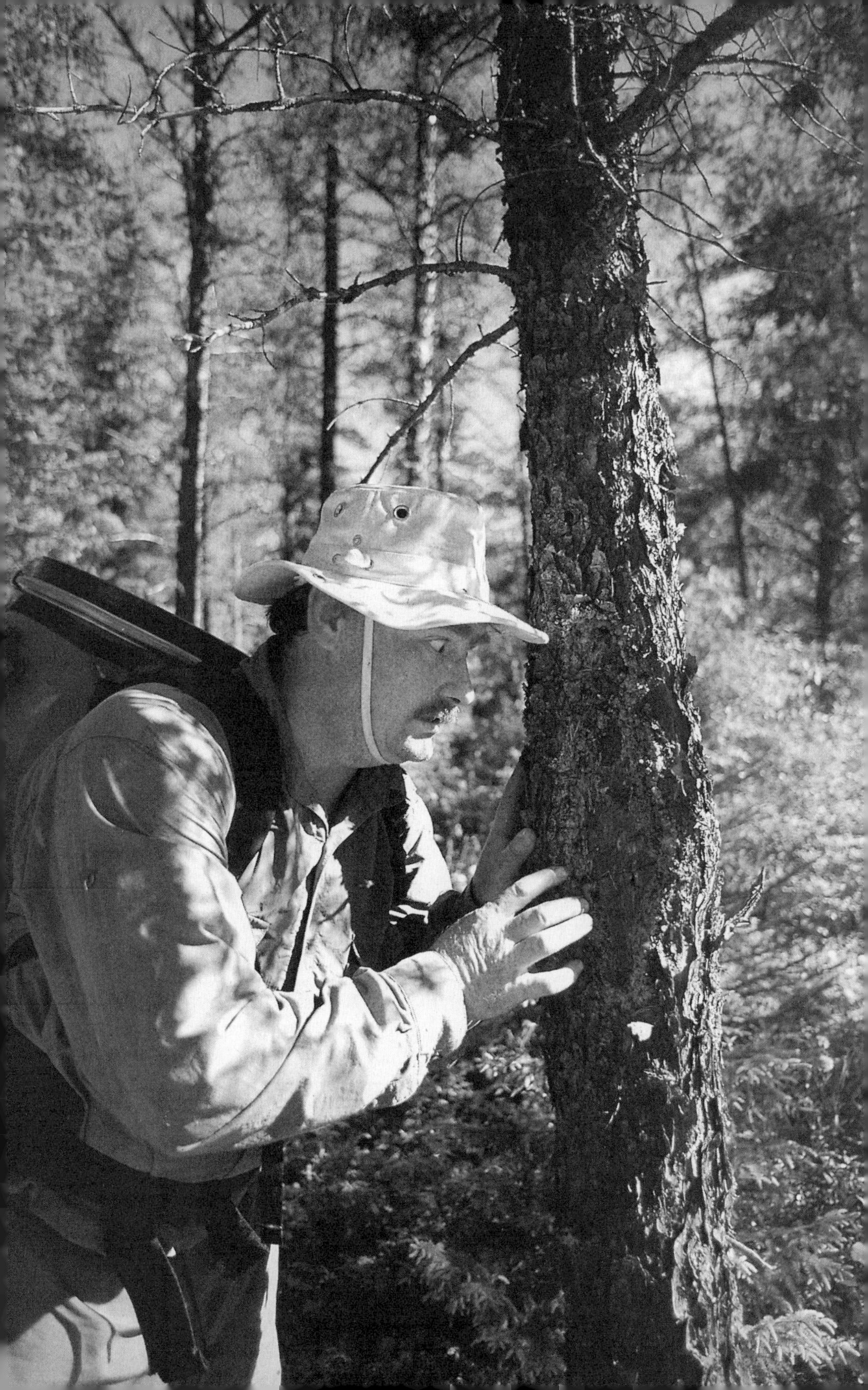

NABAKWASI
RIVER LOOP

IT WAS ALL A LAST-MINUTE ACT when canoe mate Andy Baxter and I decided to head up to the Gogama District for a quick week of fishing. We hadn't researched our trip properly and found ourselves having to choose between two routes — the Nabakwasi River and the Four M Circle Route — minutes before our planned departure. To help our decision, however, we did what any ordinary angler would do. Andy and I asked a local fly-in outfitter which he preferred — and then chose the opposite, believing in the theory that anywhere an outfitter declares is impossible to canoe to is most likely a cakewalk and where they claim there's no fish usually holds the motherlode. We ended up on the Nabakwasi.

To access the route we turned right off Highway 144 and onto Highway 661 to reach the Minisinakwa Lake public launch, which is on the left just before the town of Gogama. Parking was available here, but to play it safe Andy and I opted to store our vehicle at the Ministry of Natural Resources office, located a short distance down the highway.

The paddle northeast, across Minisinakwa Lake, was relatively uneventful. It took us under an hour to pass by the two center islands and then make a sharp right to enter the Noble River. Even what remained for the rest of the afternoon was easy work. The left fork, leading to Duckbreast Lake, was an obvious route choice even though we were told we'd mistakenly go right and end up on Pensyl Creek. And the two portages taking us to Groves Lake (160 meters to the left and 180 meters to the right) were both good trails. Andy and I even caught a few medium-size pike while crossing Groves Lake and set up camp on a gorgeous island site situated on the far end.

"I think the portage is this way, Kevin" (Andy Baxter, Togo Rapids Portage).

96 ONTARIO'S LOST CANOE ROUTES

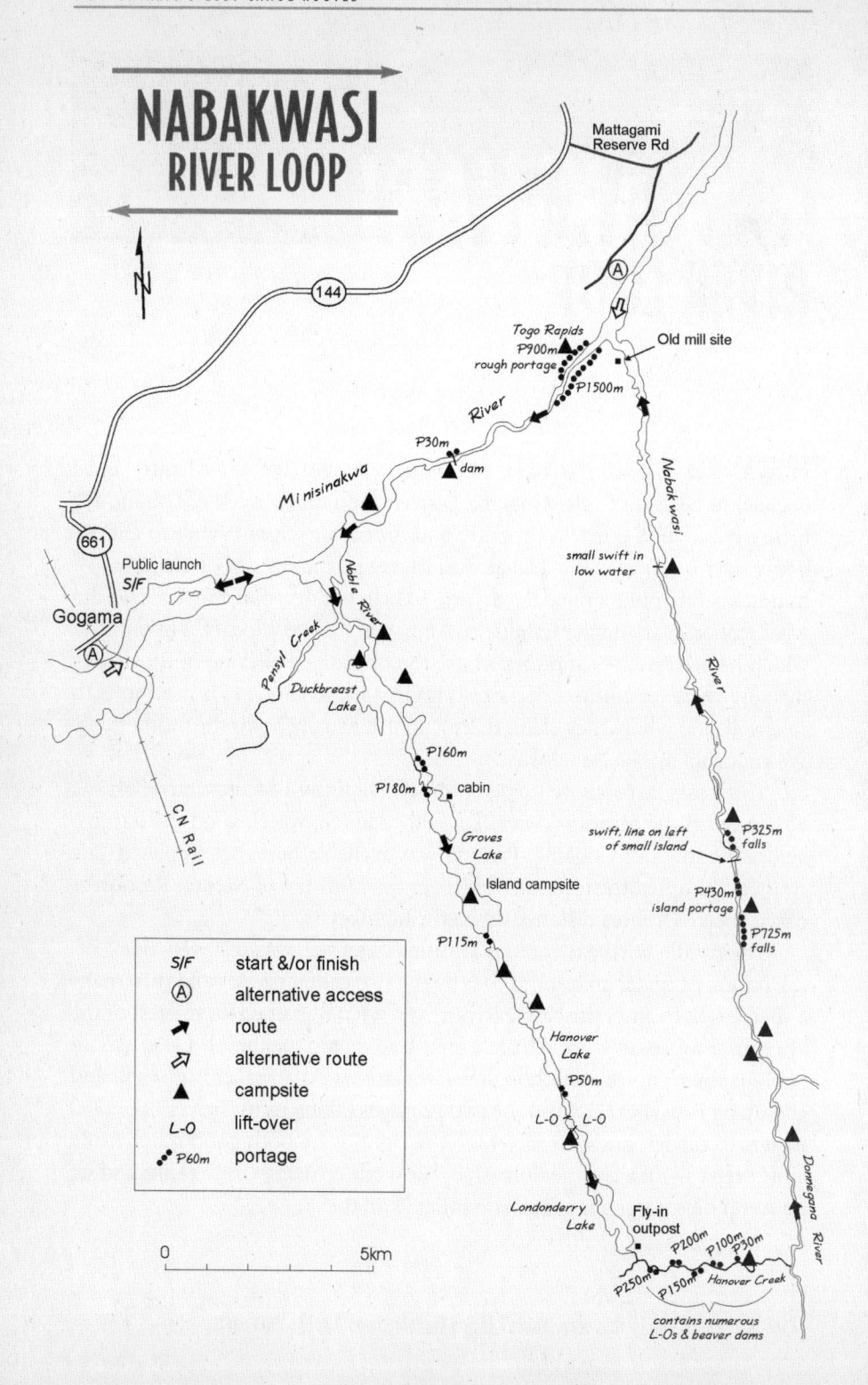

ONTARIO'S LOST CANOE ROUTES

Alana and I disembark yet again to wade another set of shallow rapids along the Chapleau River.

ONTARIO'S LOST CANOE ROUTES

Giant 300-year-old pine and hemlock are the main attraction at Marten River Provincial Park and its neighboring Nippissing Crown Game Reserve.

ONTARIO'S LOST CANOE ROUTES

Top: Once on Bark Lake, you can paddle an entire week without ever revisiting the same bay or inlet twice. It's an absolute paradise.
Bottom: The Chiniguchi River system has a landscape similar to that of Killarney Provincial Park and, surprisingly, is unknown to most canoeists.

ONTARIO'S LOST CANOE ROUTES

Top: Bagsverd Lake is typical of most lakes in Gogama. It's away from the crowds, has a scattering of small islands to camp on, and is teeming with pike and walleye.
Bottom: Temagami contains 2,400 kilometers of canoe routes and still doesn't receive the huge numbers of paddlers that Algonquin and Killarney do.

ONTARIO'S LOST CANOE ROUTES

My canoe partner, Scott Roberts, caught the smallest fish on the Dunlop Lake trip (a speckle trout just over 3 pounds) and was forced to do dishes last night out.

Top: The York River makes a perfect weekend trip; of course, that's if you don't have a stupid dog like Bailey who decides to take a swim above the largest waterfall in the district.
Bottom: Alana and I prepare to haul the canoe and gear around the first of many logjams blocking the lower portion of the Steel River.

ONTARIO'S LOST CANOE ROUTES

Drying one's boots around the evening fire became a nightly ritual while our group made our way up the West Aubinadong River.

Top: Togo Rapids, Minisinakwa River
Bottom: Finding a cozy bush site was one of the highlights of being on the remote Tatachatipika River.

The route obviously didn't match the description given to us by the local outfitters, and when we saw the company fly in a group of fishermen we couldn't help but drop our trousers and moon them as they passed overhead. It seemed only fitting, since their name was Derry-Air Outfitting.

Andy and I did have to humble ourselves a little the next morning while we made our way over to Hanover Lake. The 115-meter portage was quite steep and ended in a wide marsh. The Londonderry Lake portage (50 meters) was even steeper and included two beaver dams that required lifting over before we entered the main portion of the lake. Still, it wasn't that bad and we were quite surprised to see another group of fishermen staying at a second fly-in outpost camp at the south end of Londonderry Lake. We were even more surprised, however, when they aggressively approached us and demanded that we leave *their* lake immediately.

We didn't bother arguing with them. Actually we just ignored them completely. Andy and I figured that the outfitters themselves had misinformed the fishermen and we would be wasting our time trying to explain how absurd that idea really was. It was quite satisfying, however, that a monster pike grabbed onto my line the moment we passed by their boat.

To the right of the outpost camp was the entrance to Hanover Creek, which soon splits into two channels. Andy and I headed left and then spent the next three hours making our way to the Nabakwasi River, lifting over a total of twelve beaver dams and either lining, wading or portaging around a series of rapids.

The first marked portage (250 meters) wasn't far after a bend in the creek. It was fairly flat, marked on the right, and bypassed two sets of rapids. But the next three portages (200 meters on the left, 150 meters on the right and 100 meters on the left) were well grown over. They weren't all that necessary, however. Each section of fast water was easier to walk through than carry around. The last portage (30 meters) was essential, though, since it avoided a miniature falls along the left bank.

Hanover Creek soon flushed into Donnegana River, which eventually flushed into the Nabakwasi River. It was a boring paddle here, with most of the shoreline made up of swamp grass and old jack pine clear-cuts. But we enjoyed plenty of moose sightings (a total of two bulls and a cow with twin calves). And it didn't seem to take long for the banks to change over from lowland swamp to uplifted rock.

With such an abrupt transition, however, we were forced to get out and portage once again. The trail, marked to the right, measured a total of 725 meters and avoided a large waterfall, followed by a long section of Class I

Togo Rapids, Minisinakwa River.

rapids. Because it was getting late in the day, though, Andy and I agreed to just carry around the falls and set up camp. (Watch your footing where the portage heads uphill and then makes a steep descent near the base of the cascade.)

It was Andy's turn to cook dinner the second night out. So while he prepared the meal, I took our canoe down to the put-in, paddling the Class I rapids rather than making use of the remaining portage. I then returned to an elaborate meal of baked ham (marinated in a sweet and sour sauce) and lemon meringue pie. We could have done without the pie, and the marinated ham, for that matter, and just packed more lightweight dehydrated food. But for Andy, good-tasting, nutritional meals are an integral part of a canoe trip. For him, food is more than a simple means to an end — it is an expression of how easily one can cope in the bush and how good life could be out here.

Andy's philosophy of canoe tripping (not to mention his exceptional cooking talents) makes it wonderful to travel with him. A large part of my paddling season I find myself guiding greenhorns or at least being the appointed know-it-all of the group. Tripping this way rarely allows me to cultivate my skills, however. At times I even find myself joining the people traveling with me in cursing the rigors of the trip instead of enjoying its pleasures. But when I'm with Andy, a far more skilled woodsman than myself and a much more patient person when dealing with the hardships of canoe tripping, I tend to come back with a more positive attitude.

Such a disposition helped considerably when we made our way through the shallows of Hanover Creek. But maintaining a favorable outlook would become even more essential the next day, when we continued downriver.

Most of the Nabakwasi was okay. There were only two more portages (430 meters and 325 meters) to take directly after our campsite. The first was situated on the right side of a large island, surrounded by rapids and significant rock-shelves. The second was marked to the right of an impressive waterfall — take note that the incline toward the put-in can be quite treacherous when wet. Between the two portages we also had to line the canoe down to the left of a small island that had fast water on both sides.

The rest of the Nabakwasi we made our way along with the sluggish current, moving past large sections of marsh or alongside massive cliffs. It was far more scenic than the upper reaches, and Andy and I even took time out to explore the ruins of an old lumber mill taken over by a large birch grove. Little remained of any structures. But the entire western point, where the Nabakwasi curved to the left and then emptied into the Minisinakwa River, was made up of half-rotten slabs of wood.

It's rumored that the mill site was a regular hangout for Big Joe Laflamme — a renowned character of Gogama who supposedly had the ability to tame wild animals. His talents had him driving a pack of timber wolves down New York's Broadway Boulevard and showing moose and bears at the Canadian National Exhibition in Toronto. In 1928 he also provided three wolves for a Hollywood movie and then made his own debut in the short film *Forest Commandos*.

It was after visiting the ruins and then following the left shoreline, up the Minisinakwa River to the Togo Rapids that Andy and I faced the biggest challenge of the trip. Our map indicated that we had two portages to choose from here: a 1,500-meter trail on the left, which used an old logging road, or a more "scenic" route to the right, measuring only 900 meters.

We chose the second option. The problem was that it didn't exist. A faint path did head out from the take-out but soon was so overgrown that we found ourselves making our own route.

Loaded with the two main packs, we crashed through the thick brush for a good hour and managed to only reach the halfway point. Here we made the decision to leave the packs behind, head back to the take-out, and then carry the canoe and food barrel along the other portage on the opposite bank.

Prime moose habitat along the Donnegana River.

Our plan seemed reasonable — at least until we climbed up the steep rise to begin walking along the old road. There we discovered that a previous windstorm had toppled an entire forest. Poplar trees were scattered like toothpicks across the trail, and if weren't for the Junior Rangers (a government youth group) having recently cut out the worst sections with a chainsaw (they must have gone through gallons of gasoline), it would have been impossible to make it through.

It was just over an hour before we reached the put-in and took another hour to paddle across and walk back to our packs. By then it was pitch dark, and we ended up crawling into our tent, set up on a mound of rock adjacent to the river, and literally collapsed for the night.

Come morning we were still feeling the effects of the day before's bushwhacking. Mercifully, however, the last day out was an easy one. We had only to line up a short section of rapids just after the put-in, paddle up the remaining 2 kilometers of the Minisinakwa River to reach the 30-meter portage to the right of a concrete dam, and then head west across Minisinakwa Lake. At around 12 p.m. we found ourselves back at the public launch, and there to greet us, as we walked up to retrieve our vehicle from the Ministry of Natural Resources parking lot, was the owner of Derry-Air Outfitters.

Andy and I panicked at first, thinking he was going to bawl us out for mooning him on Groves Lake. He made no mention of our indecent act, though. The owner just wanted to hear how unpleasant our trip was and most likely expected us to tell him that he was right about the route. But we kept to Andy's positive-attitude philosophy and made no mention of how difficult Hanover Creek was to navigate or how insane the portages were around Togo Rapids. We just told tales about the fish we caught, the moose we sighted, the delicious meals we devoured, and even remarked on how gorgeous the moon was while we camped out on Groves Lake.

NABAKWASI RIVER LOOP

TIME 3–4 days

NUMBER OF PORTAGES 14

LONGEST PORTAGE 1,500 meters (900-meter alternative portage)

DIFFICULTY Intermediate canoe-tripping skills are necessary.

ALTERNATIVE ACCESS To use a second boat launch in Gogama, drive through the town (Miller Street) and take the first left past the railway crossing. Another alternative take-out is at the public boat launch on Minisinakwa River, which can be reached by turning right off Highway 144, north of Gogama, onto Mattagami Reserve Road.

ALTERNATIVE ROUTE To eliminate portaging around Togo Rapids, shuttle a vehicle from the Gogama put-in to the Minisinakwa River public boat launch.

OUTFITTERS

SUNDOG OUTFITTERS CORP.
Box 1014
Dowling, Ontario
P0M 1R0
705-855-0042
e-mail:
sundog.amorak@sympatico.ca
www.sundogoutfitters.com

FOR MORE INFORMATION

MINISTRY OF NATURAL RESOURCES
Box 129, Low Ave.
Gogama, Ontario
P0M 1W0
705-894-2000

TOPOGRAPHIC MAPS
41 P/11 & 41 P/12

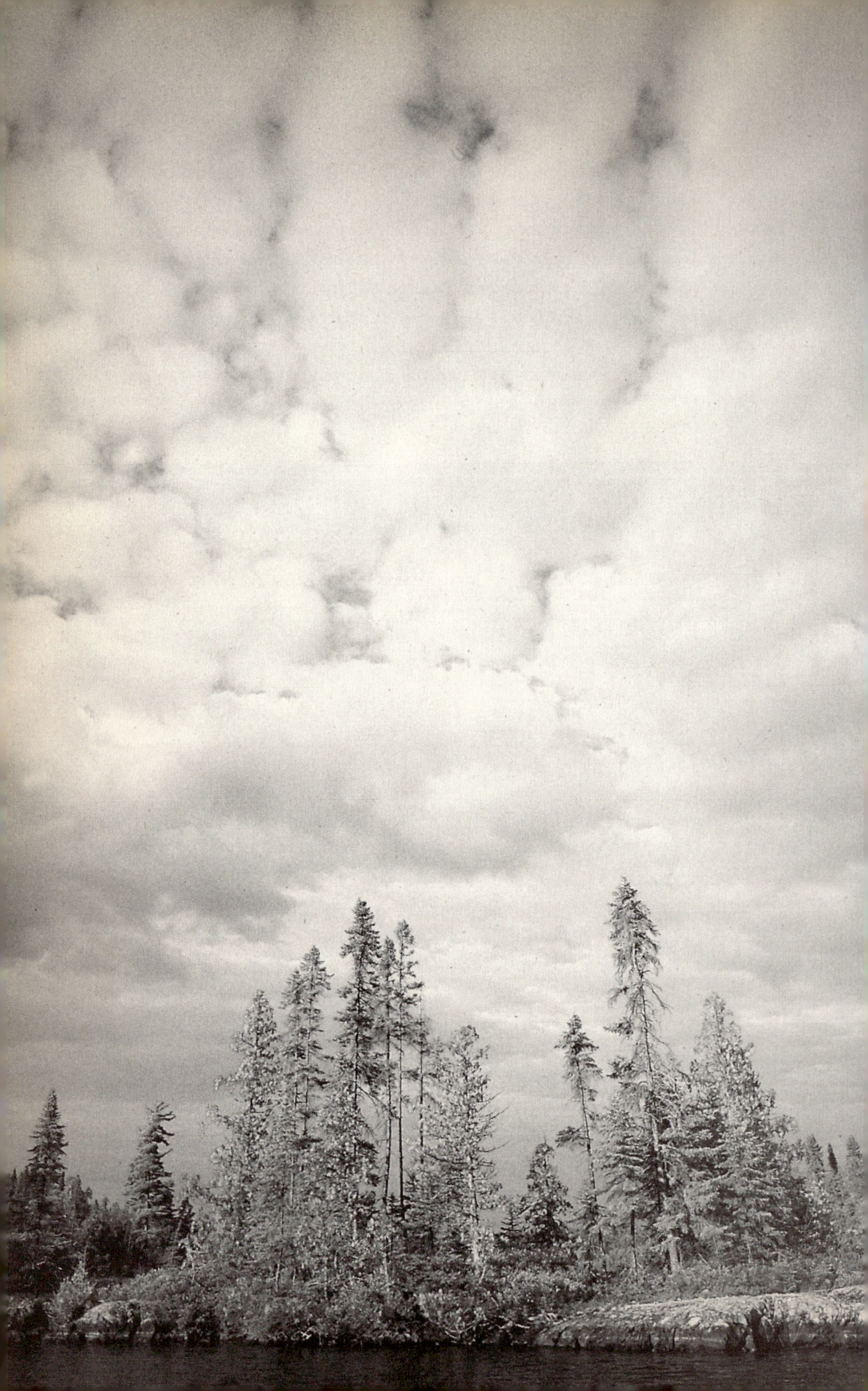

FOUR M
CIRCLE LOOP

AFTER SURVIVING GOGAMA'S NABAKWASI RIVER with partner Andy Baxter (see previous chapter), I decided only a week later to investigate the Four M Circle canoe route — a short trip located almost directly across the highway. It was said to be a much easier version of what Andy and I had just finished (the locals even nicknamed it "the amateur hour") and it sounded ideal for another canoe mate of mine, Noel Hudson. He is the chief editor for my publishing company, Boston Mills Press, and has accompanied me on a number of weekend excursions in southern Ontario. This would be his first true northern adventure. And according to him — maybe not during the trip, but when it was all over — it wouldn't be his last.

Dividing Lake marks the beginning of the Four M Circle Loop and is reached by turning west off Highway 144, 2 kilometers north of Highway 560, onto Dividing Lake Road. The gravel road forks approximately 300 meters in from the highway. The Ministry of Natural Resources Junior Ranger Camp is to the right and the public launch is to the left.

After a long six-hour drive from Toronto, it was noon before Noel and I found ourselves heading across Dividing Lake. It was a perfect day to paddle, though, with clear skies and no wind. And it wasn't long before we'd paddled beyond the Junior Ranger Camp (you can spot an old fire-tower up on a hill behind the camp) and entered the weedy bay to the northwest that led us to the Mollie River.

After the first portage (110 meters and marked to the right) the Mollie River quickly became shallow and was littered with half-submerged boulders. By the time we reached the second portage — a short 43-meter trail found along the left bank that leads into Three Duck Lake — we had been

Island campsite, Bagsverd Lake.

FOUR M CIRCLE LOOP

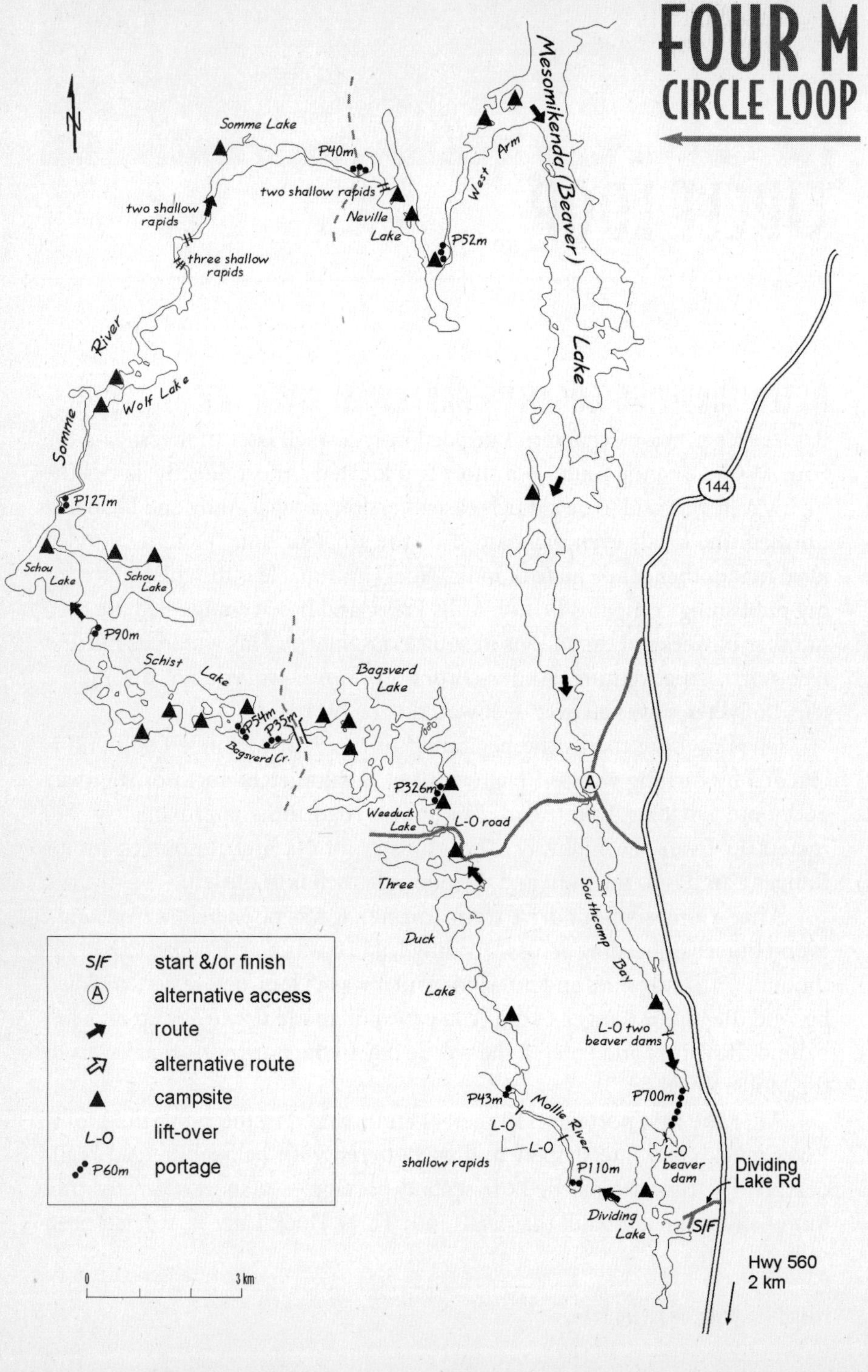

forced out of the boat twice to wade, line and lift over the debris. Eventually, however, we broke out into the open lake and continued on.

Three Duck Lake is split into three separate ponds, each linked together by two rock-strewn channels where Noel and I had to get out and drag our canoe once again. Our efforts were well rewarded, however. On each pond we trolled for pike and caught and released half a dozen fish before reaching the top end of the lake.

Our plan for our first day out was to lift over the logging road that separates Three Duck Lake with Weeduck Lake (the take-out is found just to the left of a metal culvert) and then make camp at the beginning of the 326-meter portage into the East Arm of Bagsverd Lake. Our government map had indicated a good campsite here, directly beside the ruins of a prospector's bunkhouse. (The surrounding lakes were once the center of the Gogama District's mining activity.) When we reached the site, however, not much remained of the old building, and a horde of mosquitoes were staking territory beyond the swamp adjacent to the portage. So we made a run for it. An hour later we had finished the portage and paddled our way out to the center island on Bagsverd Lake.

It was too long a day, but we still managed to cast out from our island site and reel in a few pike before bed.

By nine the next morning we were on our way again, heading up Bagsverd Creek, located on the far west end of Bagsverd Lake. The shallow stream was reminiscent of the Mollie River, but instead of rock piles to lift over, it had a number of beaver dams.

Wildlife seemed to flourish here, though. By the time we had passed under the steel-framed bridge a quarter of the way along, Noel and I had spotted a family of otter, a well-camouflaged American bittern and a mature bald eagle perched high atop a giant white pine.

Only two short portages (35 meters and 54 meters, both marked to the right) were required before we reached Schist Lake. And having dealt with the onslaught of bugs back on Bagsverd Creek, it was a pleasure to once again paddle out into the open.

Schist Lake had a number of small islands scattered about, and we tried fishing around at least half of them. The water was so discolored here, though, and the lake so shallow, averaging only about a meter, that Noel and I hooked into more stumps and rocks than fish. We soon moved on.

Finding the portage leading out of the lake, however, was even more difficult than locating the whereabouts of the fish. Our map showed it at the end of a weedy channel to the northwest. But after cruising the shoreline for over twenty minutes we found no evidence of it. By sheer luck, just as Noel and I were about to backtrack down the lake, I caught a glimpse of a weathered portage sign resting at the base of a spruce tree. The take-out soon became obvious, and the 90-meter trail, heading up and over a rocky knoll, was relatively easy, except for a few fallen trees blocking the way and a quick descent down to the put-in. The location also marked the divide between the Atlantic and Arctic watersheds. Of course, Noel and I couldn't see much difference in the landscape either way. Both were boot-sucking mud holes infested with thousands of bloodthirsty mosquitoes. But we had a swig of rum to celebrate the crossing just the same.

From here we exited a small pond and followed yet another shallow, meandering creek out into Schou Lake. The swampy stream was the worst to navigate. At times Noel had to stand up in the bow to get a fix on our direction. But when we finally reached Schou Lake both of us celebrated the open water just as before and cast out a line. Three pike later we had crossed over to the north end. Here, rather than head down the lake's southeast channel, we continued north by twisting around to the entrance of Somme River.

The 127-meter portage, marked to the right, ended in a sloppy mess, and we were forced to continue another 50 meters to reach deeper water. The river itself remained shallow and silt-ridden. Huge clumps of cattails also made progress difficult at times, and Noel and I rejoiced the moment we saw the Somme open up into Wolf Lake.

We should have stopped here. Wolf Lake had some excellent island campsites and we caught a mess of small pike in almost every weedy bay. It was still early, though, and we were set on fishing for walleye in Neville Lake before the end of the day.

The Somme River kept its character all the way to Somme Lake. On the way we lined, waded and ran the loaded canoe down three boulder-strewn rapids flushing into a pond and then two running out of it. (The second-last set could be considered a Class I technical during high water.)

Once on the far east end of Somme Lake, we then paddled under one of the four metal culverts blocking the route, took a 40-meter portage on the immediate left to avoid a medium-sized waterfall, and then turned south to flush down two more shallow rapids before entering Neville Lake.

The lake wasn't at all what we had imagined. We tried fishing for its trophy walleye below the rapids and hooked onto nothing but a giant, submerged log. Prime campsites also didn't exist. Our provincial map had two marked — one on the island directly below the rapids and another on the far east side of the center island. Both, however, had become garbage dumps,

Noel finds an old road sign pointing to Weeduck Lake. Not all the route is marked as clearly as this.

heaping with beer bottles, tin cans and, worst of all, used disposable diapers. It was truly disheartening.

To make matters worse, it began to rain. And now desperate for a place to stay, we ended up making do on a slab of rock across from the main island and dined on Kraft Dinner instead of fresh fish fillets.

The rain continued through the night and increased to a steady drizzle as we resumed the next morning. To exit Neville Lake, we headed south for a kilometer and then turned east down a narrow channel, dragging our boat over a set of shallow rapids to begin a steep 52-meter portage, marked on the left bank. And from here we entered the West Arm of Mesomikenda (Beaver) Lake, eventually veering off to the right to begin an all-day 20-kilometer paddle.

Luckily the low-lying clouds kept the wind down as we made our way south on Mesomikenda Lake. The only problem with traveling across it, apart from the boredom, was the absence of any good campsites. We did manage to check out one designated spot just after we passed under a road bridge and entered Mesomikenda's Southcamp Bay. But it was cluttered with so much garbage that we made the decision to continue on.

This was definitely a bad move. Nowhere along the remaining 5 kilometers of the lake did we find a spot to camp. So we still continued, lifting over

"Shore lunch, anyone?" Noel catches another pike while trolling across Wolf Lake.

two large beaver dams (we couldn't locate the supposed 15-meter portage that avoids them on the left) and then carrying over to Dividing Lake.

The 700-meter portage leading into the familiar Dividing Lake was a disaster zone. As Noel and I reached the top of the first rise we were met by a thick wall of fallen trees. Loggers clear-cutting on both sides of the trail were what caused the blow-downs. The company had followed protocol by leaving a 100-meter buffer zone, but this was obviously not big enough to stop the wind damage. Every 10 to 20 meters there were stacks of jack pine and spruce lying across the path. Even the trees left standing were all leaning heavily against their neighbors. It was as if the entire forest couldn't wait to tumble over.

What angered me most about the damage inflicted was that I had once worked as a forest technician in the same district some years ago. Back then we would never have crippled the forest in such a way. In fact, I remember returning to previously cut areas with workmates for a weekend of fishing or camping, neither of us feeling guilty about what we had left behind. The lumber industry had clearly changed since then. Now it was simply a case of cut and run. They should be ashamed of themselves.

To make our way to the other end of the portage, through the numerous deadfalls and eroded gullies, Noel and I had to search to the right and then to the left of the jams, looking for a way around. Most of the time there was no conspicuous trail at all, just thick bush overwhelmed by mosquitoes and blackflies, and it became easier to just drag our canoe and gear directly over or under all the debris. Then, just when we were thinking the worst was over, the moment we cleared the last pile of logs, a heavy rain began to pour down.

By the time we pulled over the beaver dam separating a small pond and Dividing Lake, it was 7:30 p.m., much too late to make a run for our vehicle parked at the access point. Instead, we made camp on the larger of two islands on Dividing and soothed our wounds with the remainder of the rum.

In retrospect, had we but known that the last portage was blocked by debris, Noel and I could have planned to shuttle a second vehicle at the public launch on Mesomikenda Lake. This would have taken away the advantage of the route forming a complete circle but it would have kept us sane at the end of the trip.

FOUR M CIRCLE LOOP

TIME 4–5 days

NUMBER OF PORTAGES 11

LONGEST PORTAGE 708 meters

DIFFICULTY Novice to intermediate canoe-tripping skills are required, depending on portage maintenance.

ALTERNATIVE ACCESS The public boat launch on Mesomikenda Lake, located a few kilometers north of Dividing Lake Road, off Highway 144.

ALTERNATIVE ROUTE The route can be shortened half a day by shuttling a vehicle from the Dividing Lake access to the public boat launch on Mesomikenda Lake.

OUTFITTERS

SUNDOG OUTFITTERS CORP.
Box 1014
Dowling, Ontario
P0M 1R0
705-855-0042
e-mail: sundog.amorak@sympatico.ca
www.sundogoutfitters.com

FOR MORE INFORMATION

MINISTRY OF NATURAL RESOURCES
Box 129, Low Ave.
Gogama, Ontario
P0M 1W0
705-894-2000

TOPOGRAPHIC MAPS
41 O/9 & 41 P/12

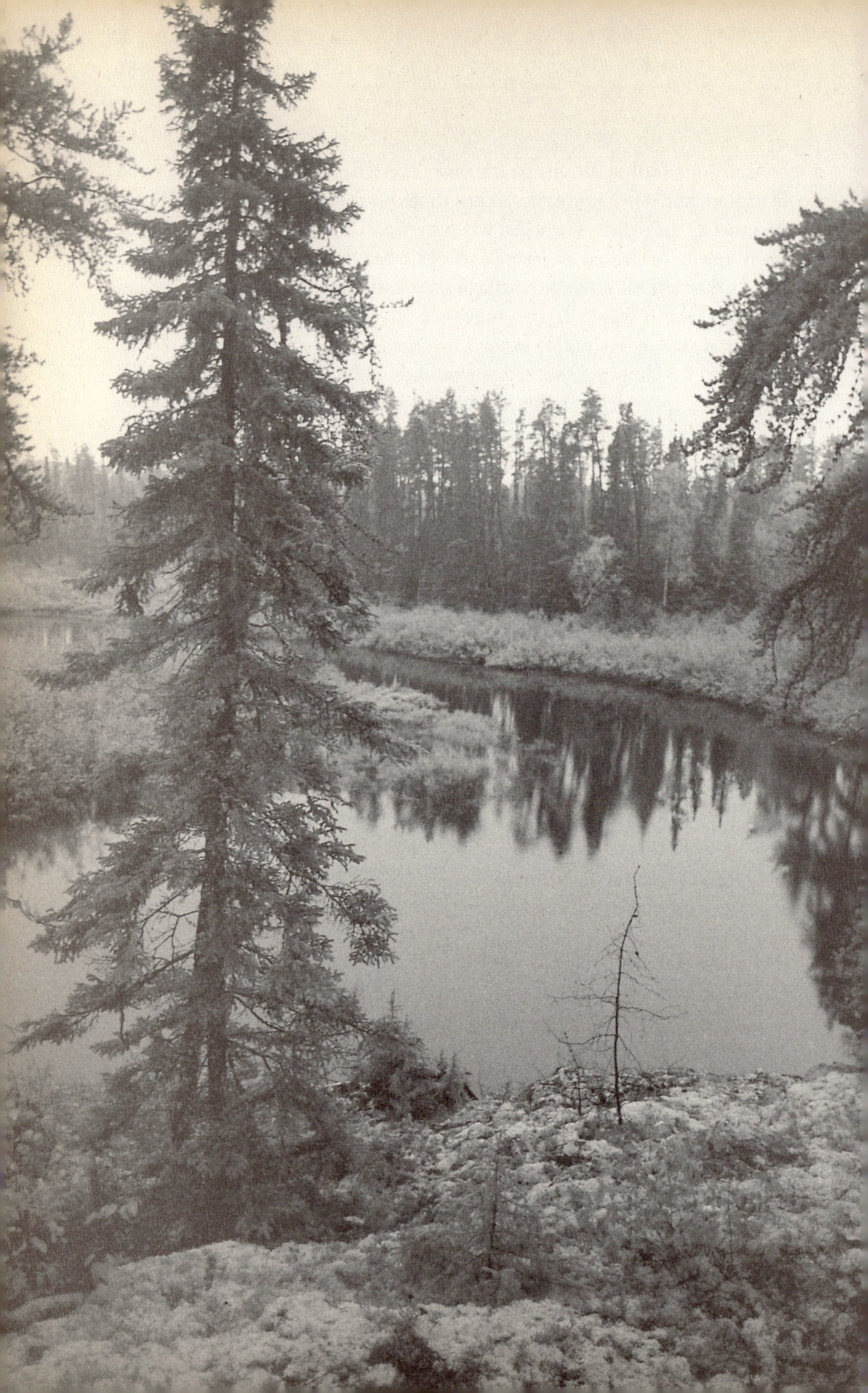

TATACHIKAPIKA RIVER

IN A WAY, MY WIFE AND I HAVE BECOME quite selfish about canoe tripping. Alana and I crave self-sufficiency and have an appetite for utter solitude. We've grown accustomed over the years to traveling alone, with only our dog, Bailey, for company. We don't have to adjust our paddling speed or alter our in-camp habits to match those of anyone else who happens to tag along. The problem, of course, is that this attitude can be dangerous at times, let alone a bit dull and somewhat unsociable — let's face it, we're borderline hermits. So we decided to invite another couple along on our next wilderness excursion.

Dave and Julie Preslie, and their one-year-old black Lab, Louie, happily agreed. We knew little about our new canoe mates except that Dave worked as a field biologist at the college where I lecture. During coffee break, Dave would always ramble on about bizarre canoe trips he and his wife had endured, some far more remote than what Alana and I had ever done. I was betting they too were wondering what it would be like to travel with another group of usually solitary canoeists.

Our route was even more unfamiliar to us. The Tatachikapika River, located southwest of Timmins, was picked for one reason. Tatachikapika is the Ojibwa word for "lost river." We just couldn't resist.

It took us a full seven hours to drive from Peterborough to the access point at Tatachikapika Lake Lodge. (Turn left off Highway 144, 32 kilometers north of Gogama.) The lodge is 8 kilometers in from the highway and, being the only development on the lake, it acts as a great starting point. The owners — Pat and Dick Neil — also offered us safe storage of our vehicles while we were on the river and agreed to shuttle them to the take-out along Highway 144 on the last day of our trip.

Upper reaches of the Tatachikapika River.

112 ONTARIO'S LOST CANOE ROUTES

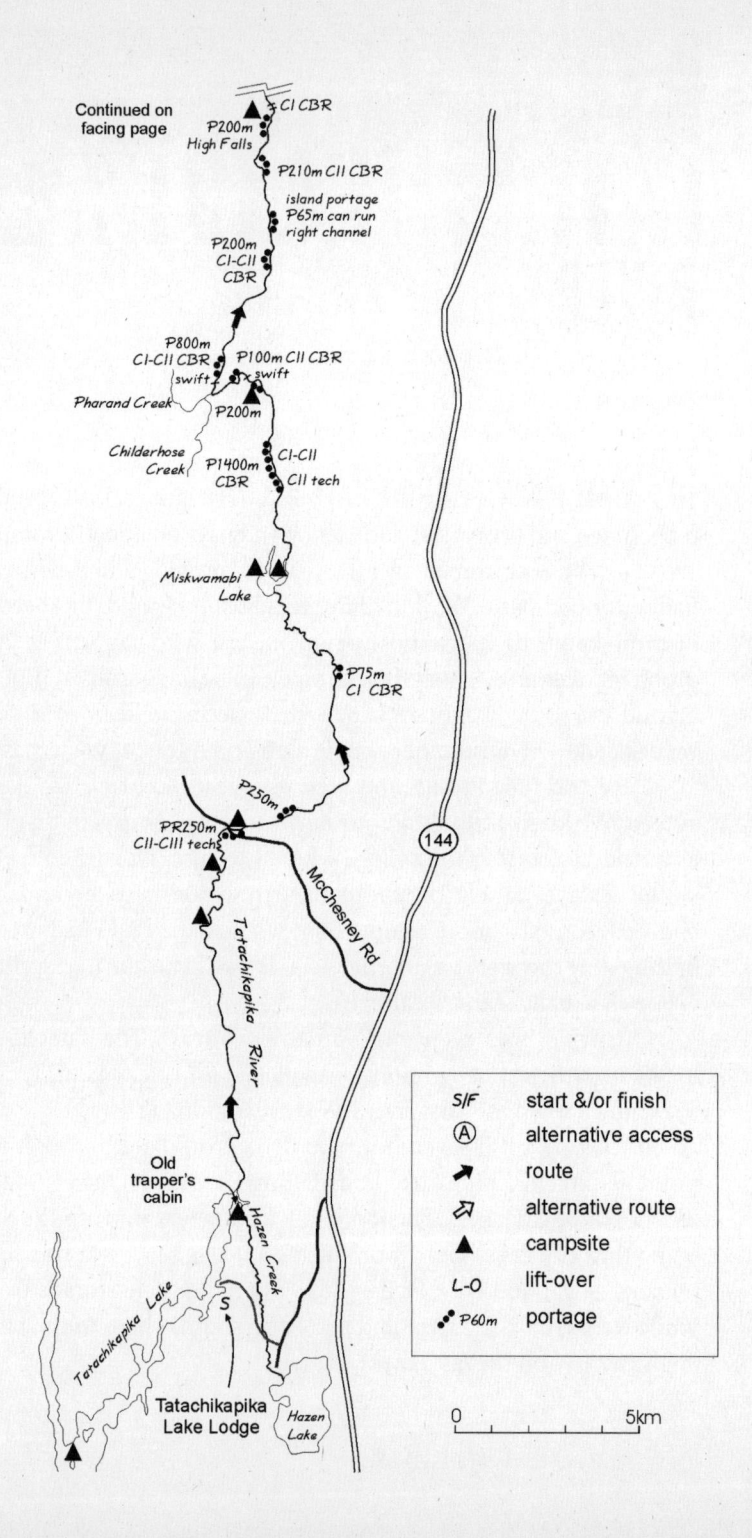

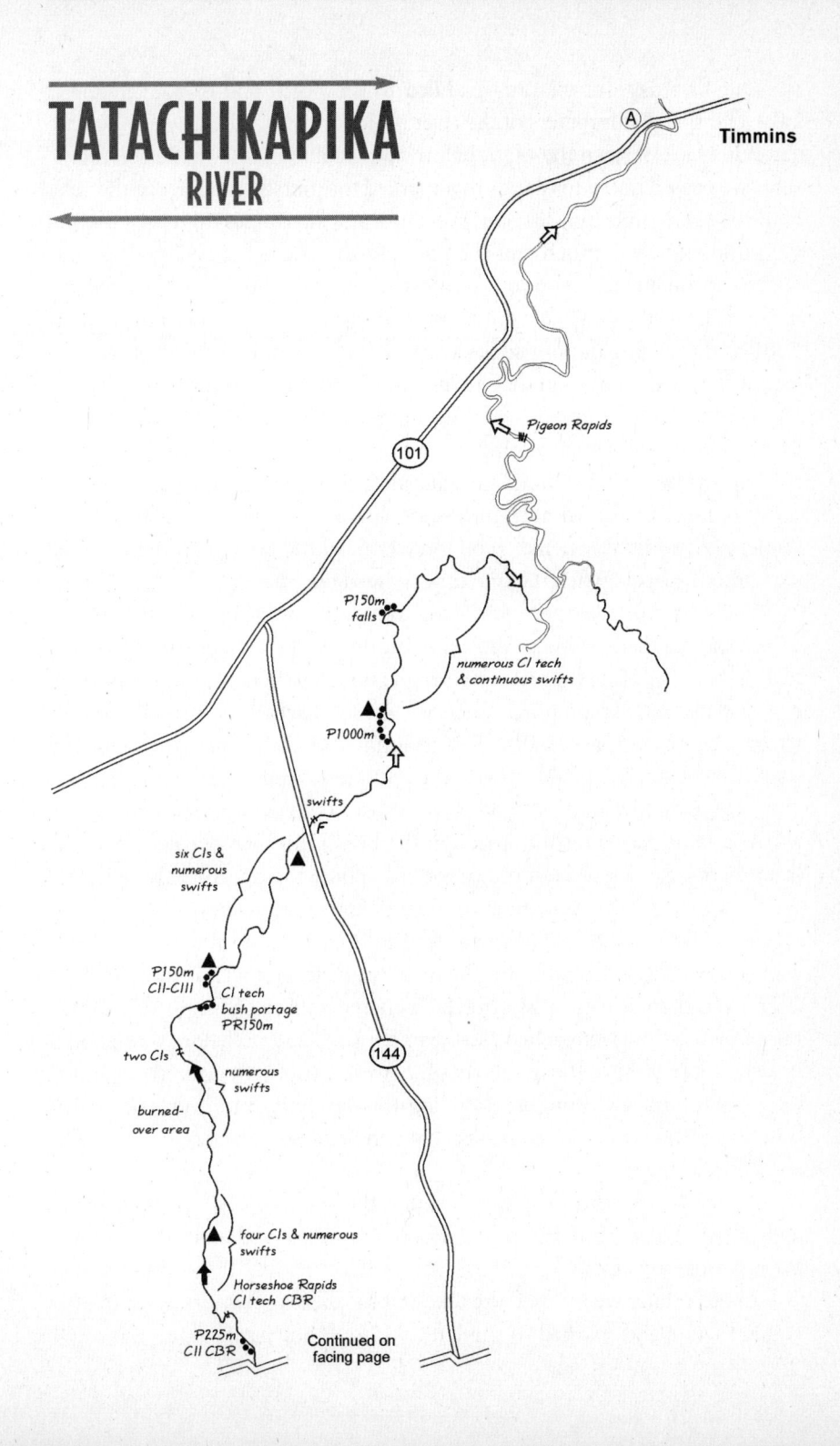

TATACHIKAPIKA RIVER

Our first day out we only paddled to the north end of Tatachikapika Lake, and then 8 kilometers of the river itself. It wasn't as far as we wanted to get. But a lack of sleep the night before and a cold rain that had been falling since we passed the twin islands that marked the marshy entrance to the river made us call it quits by 4:30 p.m. We chose a bush site, set high on a mound of granite. It wasn't much, but the two tent sites were flat and the previous tenants (probably some moose hunters in the fall) had left a pile of wood under a sheet of plastic. We got a quick fire going and, between drying our boots and wringing out our socks, cooked dinner and sipped on hot mugs of tea. By 8 p.m. the light rain had turned into a downpour, and we escaped to the tents — each group constructing a makeshift drying rack above already damp sleeping bags in an attempt to dry out gear.

We awoke to a hard rain. Our makeshift clotheslines had done little, and we were forced to crawl back into our cold, damp clothes. Even Bailey and Louie, both water dogs, had to be forced out of the tents and then coerced back into the boats when it came time to head downriver.

The dismal weather and constant meandering of the upper Tatachikapika made travel monotonous at times. The only positive note was that the rain had risen the water level high enough to float us over all fourteen beaver dams we came upon. When we finally reached the first portage en route (a technical Class II–III), all of us jumped at the chance to get out and stretch our legs. The problem was, the 250-meter trail, to the right of a logging bridge on McChesney Road, was almost nonexistent. At first we had to follow a faint path, crashing through the brush until we reached the road. From here, after a good ten minutes of searching the opposite shoulder, we finally discovered the remainder of the trail and continued on.

The next portage, a 250-meter trail to the left of an unrunnable rapid, wasn't too far downstream. But the next available spot wasn't until an hour later. Even then, it was only a quick 75-meter walk to the right of a Class I rapid. By the time we reached Miskwamabi Lake and pulled up on the public access site to have lunch, all six of us were close to hypothermia. It was only 1 p.m. but we thought of ending the day here, and even considered breaking into an abandoned trailer that had been used for target practice by some local hunters.

It was the obvious bear signs around the site that kept us moving. We enjoyed a jolt of warmth by boiling up a pot of soup and then headed out into the rain once again.

An hour later we reached the take-out for the longest portage of the trip (1,400 meters and marked to the left). We took our packs along the rough

Aware that the cold weather was numbing our reflexes and would quite possibly cloud our judgment, we agreed to portage around most of the rapids on the Tatachikapika River.

trail first, until it disappeared where a creek empties into the river. There was a slight path further on, but it became obvious that most canoeists run the rapids from at least the mouth of the creek to the base of the run. Even the section of Class II whitewater on the first half of the river looked do-able with care and careful scouting. We were all so afraid of dumping in the cold water, however, that it was decided to only flush down the last bit. And even then, rather than stepping out into the river to line through the shallow spots, we dragged our boats directly over them.

We ended our second day only 3 kilometers downstream of the last rapid, where the river takes a dramatic turn to the west. We were situated directly at the take-out of a 200-meter portage, marked to the left of another unrunnable rapid. The site happened to be the best stopover en route. But none of us took time out to notice. The rain had matured to a steady drizzle and the temperature dropped to 8 degrees Celsius (50 F). We were again desperate for a fire, and while Julie and Alana searched the backwoods for dry kindling, Dave and I erected the tarp and got a pot of tea going on the camp stove.

Surprisingly, the worst casualty of the day was Bailey. I gave her little notice at first, thinking a dog should be able to handle such foul weather. Then I saw her sitting beside the tent, shaking uncontrollably and motioning to be let inside. I finally realized the poor dog was in desperate need of warmth, and I let her nestle in among our sleeping bags.

There the frigid dog stayed until early the next morning. Even then, Alana and I had to persuade her out of the tent. It was raining again and the air temperature dropped even further, to a mere 2 degrees Celsius (40 F).

It's one thing to deal with one or two days of intermittent showers during a canoe trip. But to have it rain down hard for three solid days, and have that mixed in with extremely cold temperatures, is enough to ruin one's positive attitude toward canoe tripping for a very long time. The only thing that kept us sane was that Alana, Bailey and I weren't dealing with the mishap alone. Dave, Julie and Louie were just as miserable. Through it all though, we continued to crack jokes, tell tales of worse adventures, and even relished in the fact that our companionship grew as the trip conditions deteriorated.

We had left camp by 8:30 a.m. Around the corner we ran a small swift. But with the cold now numbing our reflexes, and quiet possibly clouding our judgment, we agreed to portage the rapids that lay further ahead. Soon we took out, just below some quick water, and began carrying 100 meters to the right of a Class II, complete with a gigantic boulder at the base of the run. And then, not long after, we also made use of a flat 800-meter portage skirting the edge of a Class I–II rapid.

The whitewater continued a couple of kilometers downstream with another good Class I–II set. And again we portaged, this time uphill for 200 meters on the left bank. (A rock garden at the base of run could cause some problems here.)

Shortly after that we did manage to flush down a side channel to the right of the small island (a 65-meter portage is marked in the center), and even portaged only the first half of the 210-trail marked to the right of the next Class II rapid. But in a way, it was a shame that we didn't run more. After all, most of the fast water en route was actually do-able with careful scouting. If it weren't for the cold temperature, I'm certain we would have relished each and every possible run rather than carry over the roughly maintained portages.

For lunch we chose the campsite situated along the steep 200-meter portage marked to the left of High Falls (an unimpressive drop of 3 meters). Hot soup was the special of the day again, to help warm our insides, and then we continued on downriver. The next section of the Tatachikapika — now

Not wanting to get their feet wet, Dave and Julie grind their way down yet another shallow swift.

protected as a Conservation Reserve through Ontario's Living Legacy — changes its character here. There was only one portage (225 meters), to the left of a Class II rapid. The rest of the river was made up of almost continuous shallow swifts and rocky Class I rapids. So we spent the entire afternoon making our way down the quick water. Because the constant rainfall had created high water levels, we rarely had to get out of our boats to avoid the gravel bars and half-submerged boulders that could easily make this river unrunnable by late June.

However, we did get out to check two sections: Horseshoe Rapids, a technical Class I approximately 3 kilometers downstream of High Falls; and a voluminous Class I with a 150-meter bush portage on the right, just before the last marked portage before the highway take-out.

The finale portage (a 150-meter trail to the left of a Class II–III rapid) was where we made camp our last night out. Clearly we hadn't meant to travel that far — a total of 29 kilometers. We had actually planned to stop at another designated site, three-quarters of the way downriver. A minor forest fire that burned both banks of the Tatachikapika River for 2 or 3 kilometers, however, had recently wiped out that site.

The portage site was worth the extra paddling, though. By the time we finished dinner, even the skies cleared a little, the rain reduced to a fine mist.

Weathering out another rainstorm on the Tatachikapika River.

And by morning we actually saw the sun. It was an incredible sensation — so much so that we hung around camp until noon. A continuous pot of coffee was placed on a bed of hot coals, ropes were strung through the trees to hang out our wet gear, and, taking a cue from Louie and Bailey, we each found our own sun spot to relax in and soak up the warmth.

Eventually we left camp and slowly made our way down to the take-out east of the Highway 144 bridge, making the most of what remained of the whitewater in the last 5 kilometers. (Half a dozen quick rapids exist right up to the highway.) Obviously none of us wanted the trip to end. We even unpacked the food barrel at the take-out and shared a late lunch together rather than drive off in search of store-bought potato chips and soda pop. Alana and I handed out some leftover cheese and bannock, Dave and Julie cooked up a can of baked beans, and the remaining dog biscuits were given to Bailey and Louie.

It was then that I realized how successful our trip really was. Any group, especially those who are unfamiliar with one another, are destined to undergo stress while dealing with such wretched weather. Major flare-ups are almost inevitable. Even minor irritants are certain to turn a trip sour. Our group, however, exhibited nothing remotely close to this.

Throughout the four days we shared on the river, our canoes traveled in close proximity, we aided one another on each and every portage, made group decisions on where to camp, actually indulged in sharing chores, and even politely debated our whereabouts when the map didn't necessarily match up with the surrounding landscape.

Noticeably, both groups had preferred paces, different levels of skill, and varied stamina. Even the dogs differed when it came to obedience in the canoe. But we managed to find a middle ground each and every time. It was enough to convince both groups to travel together again sometime.

TATACHIKAPIKA RIVER

TIME 3–5 days

NUMBER OF PORTAGES 13

LONGEST PORTAGE 1,400 meters

DIFFICULTY This is a perfect river route for intermediate whitewater paddlers.

ALTERNATIVE ACCESS McChesney Road bridge makes a good alternative put-in, and the public launch in the town of Timmins can be used as a second take-out.

ALTERNATIVE ROUTE The first section of the Tatachikapika River is quite meandering and can be avoided by taking the McChesney logging road, west off Highway 144, and accessing it at the bridge crossing. The route can also be extended two more days from the Highway 144 take-out by continuing on to Timmins. However, take note that this section of river contains numerous Class I–II rapids and is much more demanding than what's west of Highway 144.

OUTFITTERS

TATACHIKAPIKA LODGE
Box 338
Gogama, Ontario
P0M 1W0
705-894-2037
e-mail: tcpl@ntl.sympatico.ca
www.tatachikapika.gogama.on.ca

FOR MORE INFORMATION

MINISTRY OF NATURAL RESOURCES
Box 129, Low Ave.
Gogama, Ontario
P0M 1W0
705-894-2000

TOPOGRAPHIC MAPS
41 P/13, 42 A/4, 42 A/5 & 42 A/6

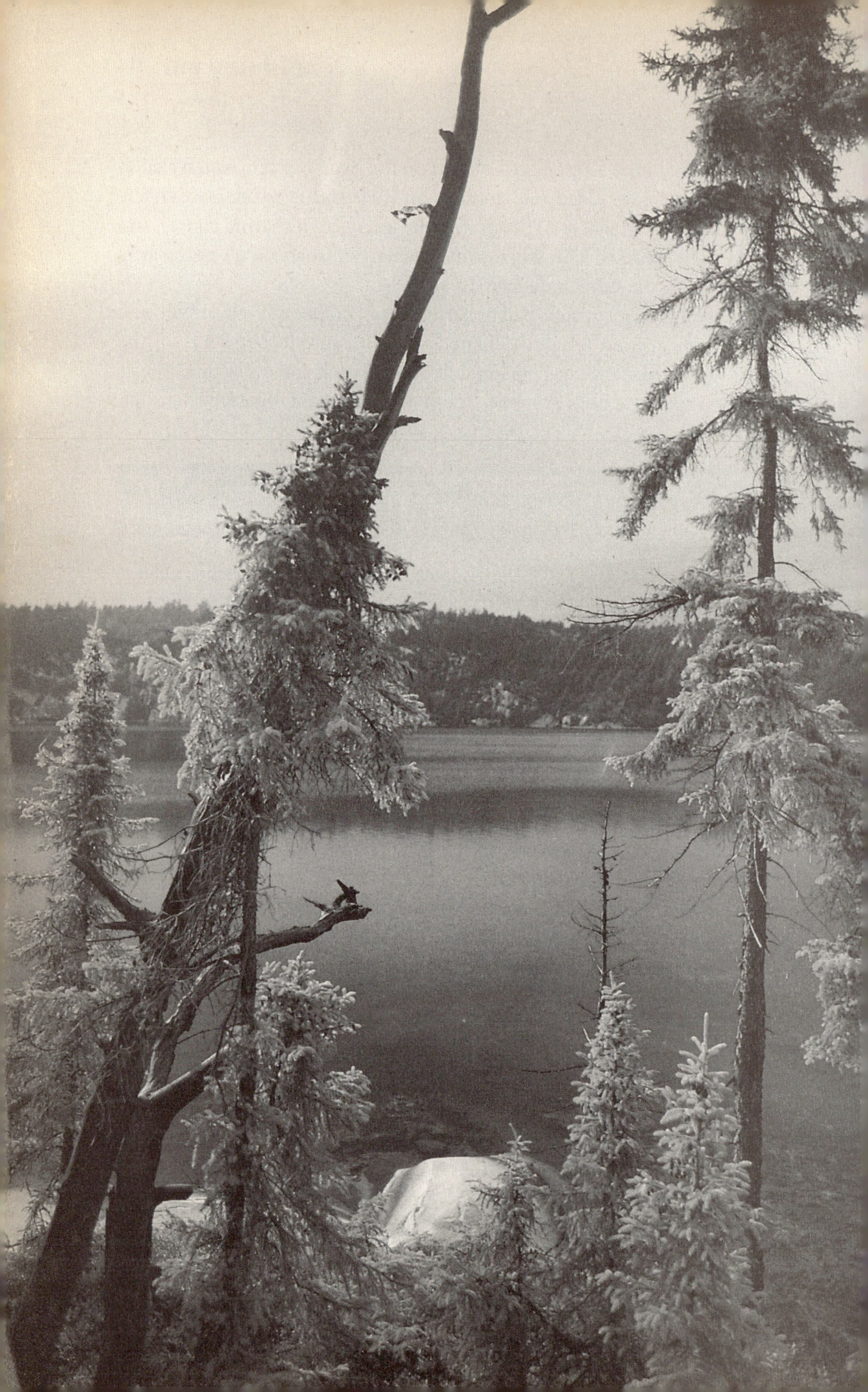

CHINIGUCHI RIVER

THE CHINIGUCHI RIVER SYSTEM is Killarney without the crowds. Killarney Provincial Park, set in Ontario's La Cloche mountain range, is a well-known canoeing area southwest of Sudbury. Its turquoise lakes and shimmering quartzite hills have attracted thousands of outdoor enthusiasts. For years it has been my favorite place to paddle. However, the Chiniguchi River, located to the east of Sudbury, has a landscape very similar to Killarney's and, surprisingly, is unknown to most canoeists. So there are times when, rather than attempt to book a site in the overcrowded interior of Killarney, I've left the frustration of the park's reservation system behind and headed out to Chiniguchi.

To reach the access point on Matagamasi Lake, follow Kukagami Lake Road north of Highway 17, located approximately twenty minutes east of Sudbury. The road is gravel, with quite a bit of washboard, but it's still manageable for most vehicles.

The first main fork in the road is at the 22-kilometer mark. Go left here and follow Matagamasi Lake Road for another 5 kilometers. Then head right and drive for another 1.4 kilometers (make sure to keep to the right when the road splits three ways) to reach the poorly maintained government launch on the south end of Matagamasi Lake. Some canoeists continue past the second turnoff and either access 5 kilometers further on, using an unmarked put-in on the right, or even drive all the way (19 kilometers) to the bridge between Wolf and Dewdney Lake. The road gets rougher the further you go, however, and I would strongly advise that you stick to the first or second access point.

From the government launch you can choose from several trips, ranging from a quick weekend outing on Maskinonge Lake to the extensive Sturgeon River Loop. The best overall tour, however, is the paddle to Chiniguchi Lake

The Chiniguchi River system offers everything that you'd find in popular Killarney Provincial Park – but without the crowds.

ONTARIO'S LOST CANOE ROUTES

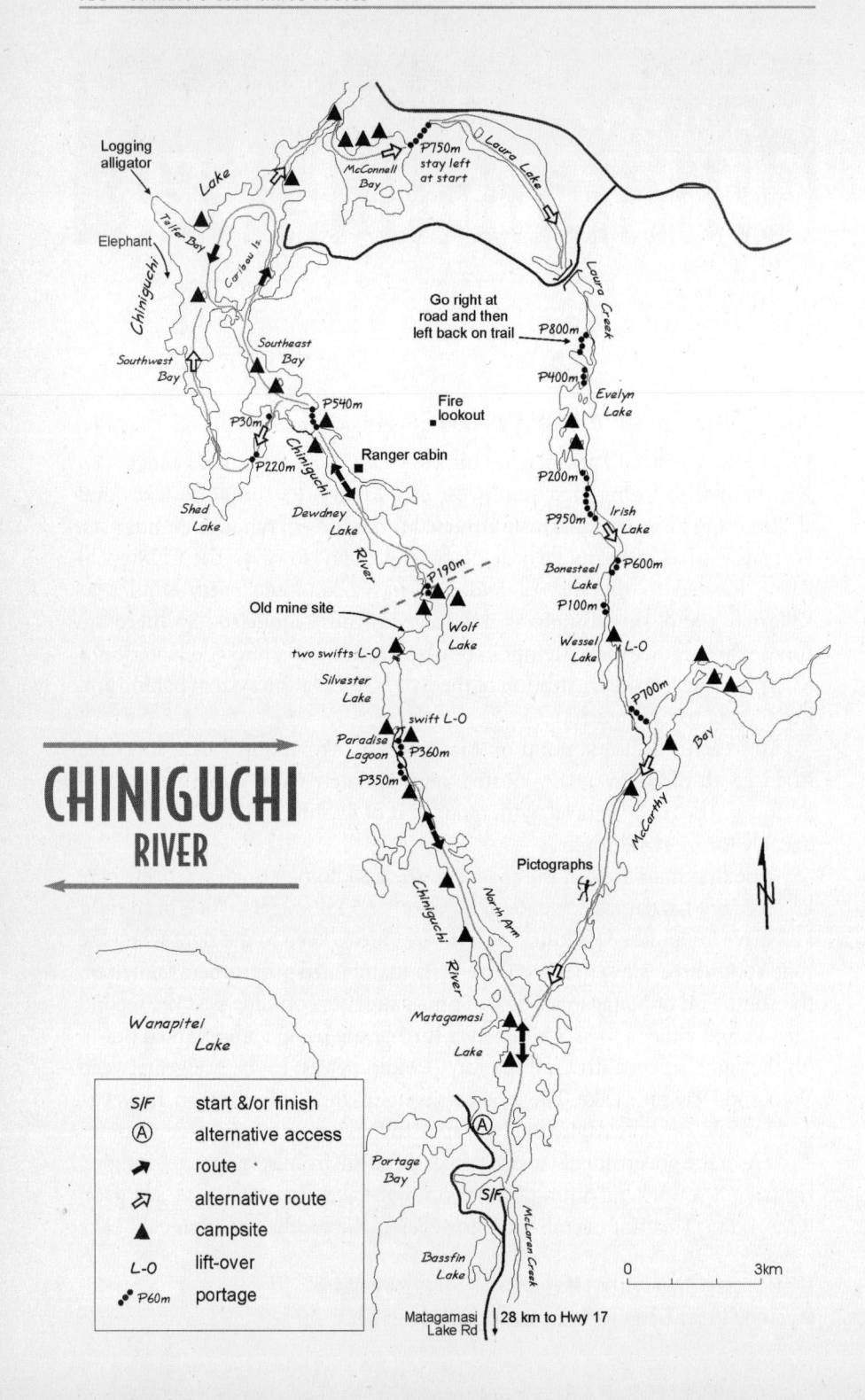

CHINIGUCHI RIVER

Map labels:

- Logging alligator
- Telfer Bay
- Elephant
- Chiniguchi Lake
- McConnell Bay
- P750m stay left at start
- Laura Lake
- Caribou Is.
- Southwest Bay
- Southeast Bay
- Go right at road and then left back on trail
- Laura Creek
- P800m
- P400m
- Evelyn Lake
- P30m
- P540m
- P220m
- Fire lookout
- Ranger cabin
- Chiniguchi River
- Shed Lake
- Dewdney Lake
- P200m
- P950m
- Irish Lake
- P190m
- Old mine site
- Bonesteel Lake
- P600m
- two swifts L-O
- Wolf Lake
- P100m
- Wessel Lake
- L-O
- Silvester Lake
- swift L-O
- Paradise Lagoon
- P360m
- P350m
- P700m
- McCarthy Bay
- Pictographs
- Chiniguchi River
- North Arm
- Wanapitei Lake
- Matagamasi Lake
- Portage Bay
- Bassfin Lake
- McLaren Creek
- Matagamasi Lake Rd — 28 km to Hwy 17

Legend:
- S/F — start &/or finish
- Ⓐ — alternative access
- → route
- ⇨ alternative route
- ▲ campsite
- L-O lift-over
- •• P60m portage

0   3km

and back. Begin the route by heading directly up Matagamasi Lake, following the north arm to where the first portage (350 meters) eventually appears on the left. It's a long paddle across and cottages clutter the shoreline. The white quartzite rocks and turquoise-colored lakes that invite comparisons to Killarney don't show themselves until after the first portage. But Matagamasi is still quite scenic and there are a number of prime campsites located on rock outcrops and pine-clad islands if you happen to become windbound or arrive late your first day out.

My worst experience traveling to Chiniguchi Lake actually began while I was making my way across Matagamasi Lake. It was the last trip of the season and my first outing in the area. Overall it had been a good paddling year. I had so far logged a total of fifty-four days in a canoe. However, it also rained every day except for eleven. And as I pushed myself hard against a strong northwest wind out on Matagamasi, rain began to pour down on me once again.

I had simply had it with the rain. I was fed up with scraping black mold off my rain jacket, sleeping in a damp tent, and never being able to get a decent fire going to actually dry off. And now I had to endure it all again. With the steady winds on Matagamasi, it took me a long three hours to reach the first portage. It was a relatively easy trail but the recent rain had greased up the rocks, and I ended up falling hard at the put-in. The canoe came crashing down on me and a sharp edge on the aluminum gunwale gave me a large gash on my forehead. Of course, everything packed inside my first-aid kit had become absolutely soaked and I had to resort to holding a piece of gauze over the cut with a strip of duct tape.

Basically I was having a bad day. Heck, I was having a bad year. And after my tumble at the end of the first portage I became extremely paranoid about taking on the second — a steep 360-meter trail marked on the right, almost immediately after the first portage. I took little notice of the spectacular waterfall I was walking around. In fact, I didn't even take time out to explore the infamous swimming hole found on the opposite side of the cascade, known locally as Paradise Lagoon (this oval-shaped basin is a must-see for all canoeists passing through).

After blindly completing the second portage I paddled across Silvester Lake. By then the rain had turned into a torrential downpour, and I never once looked up to take in the breathtaking scenery. Instead I hurried along, lifting over two shallow swifts that connected Silvester Lake with Wolf Lake, and then made camp on the first site I came upon. It was 7 p.m. A trip that should have taken a leisurely four hours had taken me an exhausting eight. It continued to rain and, still depressed about the weather, I decided to crawl into the mildewed tent without any supper and curled up for the night inside my soggy sleeping bag.

Early the next morning I awoke to the sound of rain pelting against the side of the tent. I was obviously reluctant to get out of bed but since I hadn't eaten anything the night before my grumbling stomach forced me to crawl out and get breakfast on the go. After cooking myself up an extra helping of flapjacks I packed up my wet gear once again and paddled off into the rain.

In the northwest bay of Wolf Lake was the first portage of the day. The 190-meter trail is marked to the right of another scenic cascade and uphill most of the way. It's a straightforward path, however, and eventually levels out where it crosses over the Matagamasi extension road. Rumor has it that the Ministry of Natural Resources is thinking of dismantling this road at the bridge crossing to keep the area less accessible. I personally think this would be a great asset if the newly proposed Chiniguchi Waterway Provincial Park and Wolf Lake Forest Reserve is established. The Wolf Lake area itself contains one of the largest remaining contiguous stands of old-growth red pine (averaging 140 years) in Ontario, and the canoe route itself is based on an ancient travelway that follows traditional portages. However, resource extraction has always been the major activity in the area. There are remnants of an old mine depot along the west shore of Wolf Lake, and a network of logging roads spreads throughout the neighboring hills. And with forestry operations remaining active in the area, and considerable mining exploration still going on, I have my doubts about the effectiveness of any proclamation of extra protection for this waterway route.

My next lake crossing was Dewdney Lake. It's divided into two main sections. There's an old ranger cabin along the east shore of the upper section of the lake. The building was once used to house the caretaker for the nearby fire tower but now accommodates only a large population of field mice and a ghost named Bob. I witnessed the field mice myself while I explored the ruins. But it was a group of kids from Camp Ahmek, who joined me for lunch on the dilapidated porch, who informed me about the apparition. Apparently Bob, the old caretaker, died a mysterious death here long ago, and his ghost remains to spook each and every trespasser.

Because of the rain, the youth group decided to camp out beside the haunted house, hoping that it was possessed only on the inside. Meanwhile, I continued on to Chiniguchi Lake by way of the 540-meter portage located on the north end of Dewdney Lake. The trail was an easy carry, and after one look at the fabulous scenery of Chiniguchi — a lake very similar to

Ridge hiking along the east shore of **Wolf Lake**.

Killarney's Threenarrows — I was glad I'd chosen to endure the rain rather than face Bob the ghost. The constant drizzle had also kept the lake quite calm, and by late afternoon I even managed to reach McConnell Bay — an inlet situated on the far northeast end of Chiniguchi that has an incredible sand beach stretched out almost a full 2 kilometers.

I spent my third day paddling down the west side of Chiniguchi Lake, exploring the remains of a logging alligator in Telfer Bay, scrambling up a quartzite ridge known as the Elephant, and then making my way through a shallow narrows to reach Shed Lake. The Ahmek kids had told me that here, an unmarked 200-meter portage into Dead Lake, plus a short 20-meter lift-over, would bring me back to the familiar Southeast Bay on Chiniguchi. The shortcut was obviously not a well-traveled route. The first portage was only marked by a few old axe blazes and had a number of trees fallen across it. The lift-over was also bushed over, and I ended up just dragging my canoe over the rocks. The portage did, however, allow me to complete a full loop on Chiniguchi and still have enough time to paddle back to my choice site on Wolf Lake for my last night out.

I left Wolf Lake early the next morning, worried about the wind conditions out on Matagamasi. On the return trip down the Chiniguchi River, I did

Easy portaging makes Chiniguchi Lake an excellent choice for a family canoe trip.

take time out to stop for a skinny-dip at Paradise Lagoon. Since it is a local hotspot, it was probably the worst place to choose to swim naked, but I tend not to pack a bathing suit on solo trips. I figure there's really no need. Besides, I think there's something to be said for skinny-dipping. It gives a simple feeling of freedom, especially in a place such as this, surrounded by cool, clear, cleansing water.

Luck would have it, though, that before I could take my first dive from the rock wall that surrounded the lagoon, it once again began to storm. So, with thunder rumbling off in the distance, I slipped back into my moldy rain jacket and continued on my way.

Now I was really depressed. I guessed my last canoe trip of the season was destined to end in the rain. Even when I decided to run the last set of rapids rather than carry over the 350-meter portage that I had injured myself on, I ended up wedging my canoe on a stack of boulders near the base of the run. By the time I freed the canoe and paddled out into the expanse of Matagamasi Lake, there was a strong south wind, forcing me to inch my way along the west shoreline, moving ever so slowly toward the boat launch on the opposite end.

It wasn't really the poor weather I was upset with. I just wasn't ready to go back in such a somber mood. Something important needed to come from my time alone out here before I was forced to pack my gear away for another long winter.

Then, three hours into the crossing, it happened. A single loon surfaced directly in front of my bow. Then another. And another. Soon there were twenty-four loons swimming around my canoe, wailing out a chorus of mournful cries. This was it. For such a moment, I would once again endure all the hardships, rain or shine.

CHINIGUCHI RIVER

TIME 2-4 days

NUMBER OF PORTAGES 8 (4 which are doubled-back on)

LONGEST PORTAGE 540 meters

DIFFICULTY This is considered a novice route.

ALTERNATIVE ACCESS An unmarked put-in on the right side of Matagamasi Lake Road, 5 kilometers past the turnoff leading to the main public launch.

ALTERNATIVE ROUTE It is possible to loop back to Matagamasi Lake from Chiniguchi Lake's McConnell Bay by following a poorly maintained route through Laura Lake – Laura Creek – Evelyn Lake – Irish Lake – Bonesteel Lake – Wessel Lake – and Matagamasi Lake's McCarthy Bay.

OUTFITTERS

SUNDOG OUTFITTERS CORP.
Box 1014
Dowling, Ontario
P0M 1R0
705-855-0042
e-mail: sundog.amorak@sympatico.ca
www.sundogoutfitters.com

PADDLE SAFE ADVENTURES
926 Beverly Drive
Sudbury, Ontario
P3E 4B5
705-522-2268
e-mail: paddlers@paddlesafe.com
www.paddlesafe.com

FOR MORE INFORMATION

MINISTRY OF NATURAL RESOURCES
3301 Trout Lake Rd.
North Bay, Ontario
P1A 4L7
705-475-5550
or
3767 Hwy. 69 S.
Suite 5
Sudbury, Ontario
P3G 1E7
705-564-7823

TOPOGRAPHIC MAPS
41 I/15

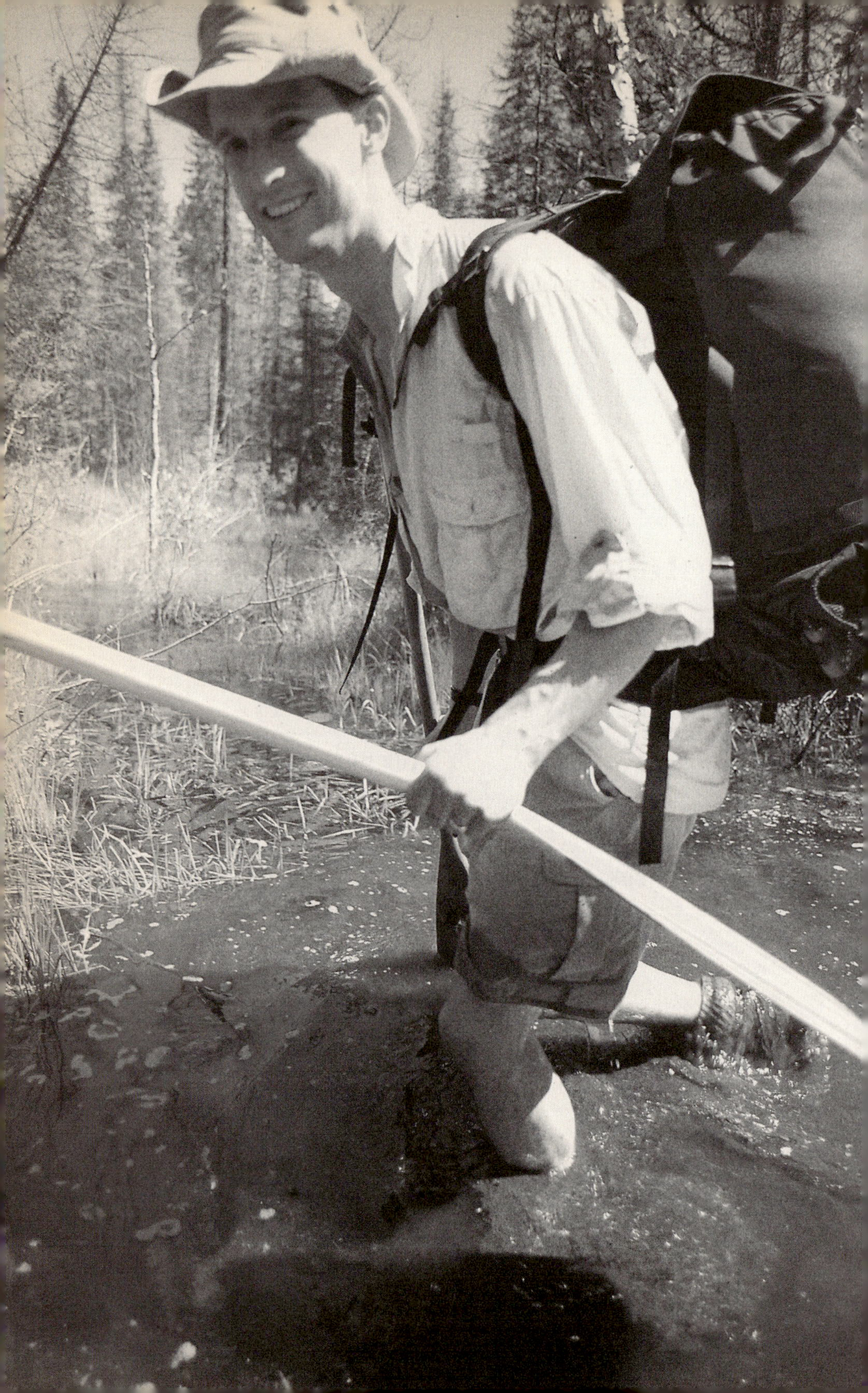

TEMAGAMI'S
CANTON LAKES

TEMAGAMI'S MAIN CANOE ROUTES have recently been showing signs of overuse. Campsites are littered with garbage, portages are cluttered with not-so-polite canoeists, and a number of historical sites have been vandalized. It's not that the area is a new frontier for canoeists. As far back as 1922, in an article in *Outdoors Recreation* magazine, David L. Holmes remarked, "We saw plenty of people while in Temagami — many more than we are accustomed to seeing up in the secluded nooks of Georgian Bay region." But now, more than ever, Temagami's main paddling corridors are becoming a bit of an eyesore.

The saving grace, however, is that Temagami still doesn't receive the huge numbers of canoeists that Algonquin and Killarney do. Even if it did, this 13,000-square-kilometer area still contains a number of remote side trips, most of which have been left off government maps. These unmarked routes — called Nastawgan (a Cree-Ojibwa word for "network of trails") — are part of an ancient trail system first established more than 1,000 years ago by the Teme-Augama Anishnabai people and are now managed by local camps and the Friends of Temagami.

Camp Keewaydin (Temagami's oldest camp) has kept up maintenance on one particular circuit, called the Thunderhead Route and known locally as the Canton Lakes. It consists of a chain of small lakes between the top end of Lake Temagami and Bob Lake, and is used on a regular basis by the Keewaydin canoe-trippers to reach a significant patch of old-growth pine located on the north end of Obabika Lake.

"Are there leeches in here?" Matt leads the way on the portage out of Stiles Lake.

130 ONTARIO'S LOST CANOE ROUTES

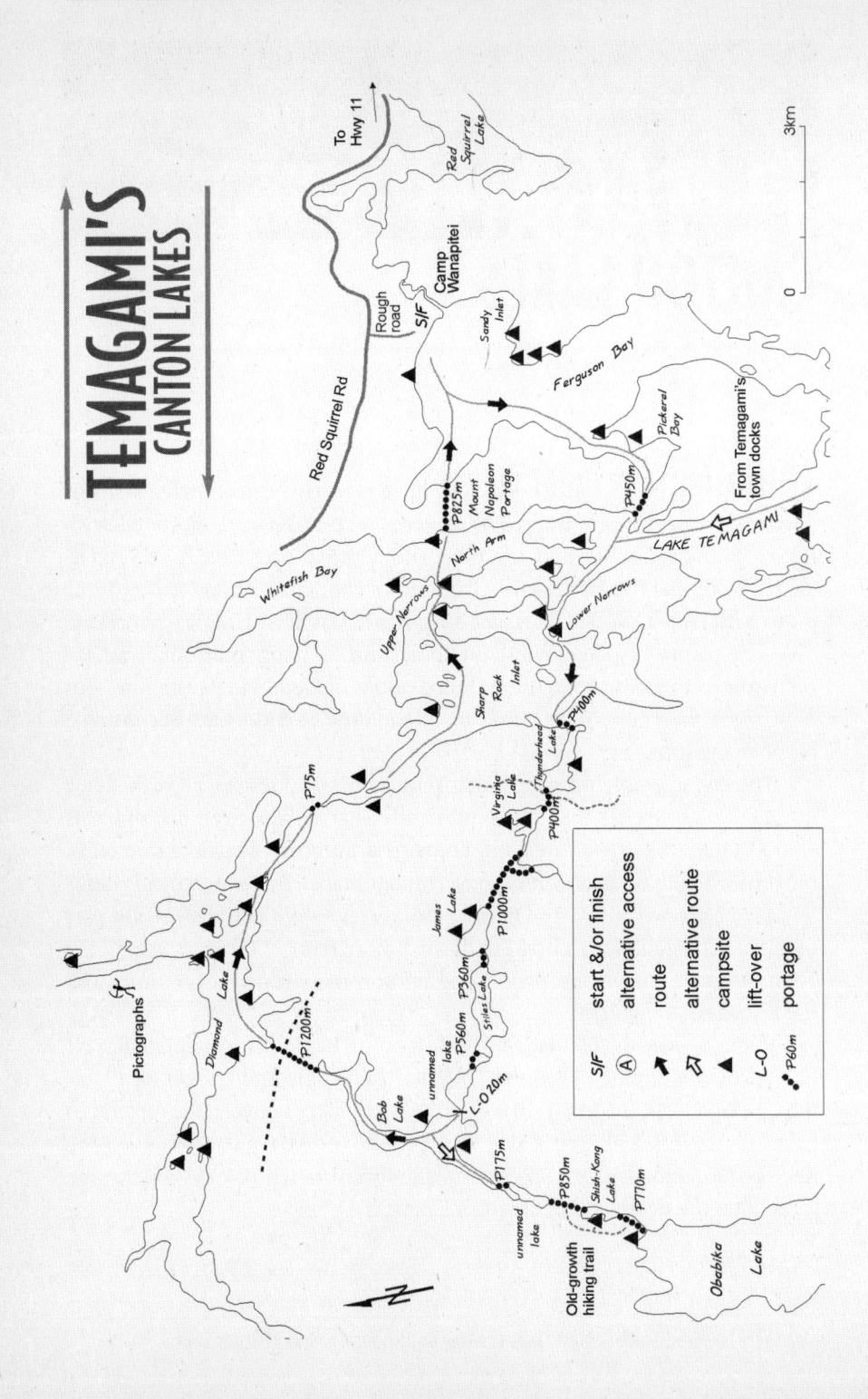

During the summer of 2000, while guiding for Wanapitei Outfitters, I was lucky enough to co-lead on a trip through the Canton Lakes. I found it one of the finest out-of-the-way circuits Temagami has to offer.

Our group consisted of the main guide, Jamie Sculthorpe; three clients, Fred Shuttleworth, Matt McPhersey, his wife, Teresa Clayton; and me. We all met the night before at the Wanapitei lodge, next to Temagami's Ferguson Bay canoe launch area. The site became a youth camp in 1931 but was initially settled by Father Charles Paradise in 1891 as a small retreat and later held an orphanage.

You could start the route from Temagami's town docks or even from the end of Lake Temagami's access road. However, this would add at least two extra days of paddling on the exposed Lake Temagami. So even if you don't plan to use the services of Wanapitei Outfitters, Ferguson Bay's Sandy Inlet is your best bet. That is, of course, if your vehicle can handle the rough ride in. The 28.9 kilometers along the Red Squirrel Road, west off Highway 11 and 10 kilometers north of Temagami, seems to be getting worse every year. But it still remains manageable for most vehicles. The last short section of side road (marked to the left) is the major problem. Deep ruts and mud-filled potholes mean that only vehicles with good clearance can make it all the way to the Wanapitei parking area. (A 200-meter portage is necessary from the parking lot to the beach adjacent to the lodge.)

Because we accessed the route from Wanapitei, our group still had to deal with the expanse of Lake Temagami's Ferguson Bay, the North Arm, and Sharp Rock Inlet before reaching the Canton Lakes. Here we had two options. First, to save us time on the open water, we could paddle directly west toward Mount Napoleon (a 1,150-meter mound of rock carved in the shape of Napoleon's hat) and take the incredibly steep 825-meter portage into the North Arm. Then, by maneuvering through shallow water of the North Arm Upper Narrows, we could reach Sharp Rock Inlet. Our second option would be to paddle southwest on Ferguson Bay to Pickerel Bay, and then take a much easier 450-meter portage to the North Arm. The Lower Narrows of the North Arm would then take us to Sharp Rock Inlet, and almost directly across we would find the first portage leading into Thunderhead Lake.

Not wanting to deal with Mount Napoleon our first day out, we opted for the longer paddle southwest on Ferguson Bay. It was a good choice. None of us had paddled together before, and the easy 450-meter portage connecting Pickerel Bay with the North Arm provided a good opportunity for us to sort out our portaging technique.

The group gathers to celebrate surviving day one of hardship.

Since Fred and I were canoe partners, we agreed to carry our canoe, personal belongings, and the food barrels. Matt and Teresa loaded up with their canoe and packs. And Jamie, the strongest of the group, managed his solo boat and the remaining Wanapitei gear. By the end of the two trips across we were quite organized. But it actually took a couple of changes mid-trail before we could sort things out, especially with Fred and me. At first I chose to shoulder a barrel of food — loaded down with such items as canned ham, half-a-dozen red cabbages, and king-sized potatoes. Fred agreed to strap on the Wanigan, full of all the heavy kitchen utensils, including a cast-iron frying pan and extra-sized reflector oven. Halfway across we both decided to switch, however. Fred favored the pain of the round plastic barrel digging into his back, while I preferred a square wooden box attached to my forehead by a tight leather tump, forcing most of the weight directly down on my spine.

By midmorning we had completed the first carry and were able to make it across the North Arm and Sharp Rock Inlet before the winds picked up much.

The take-out for the second portage — a 400-meter trail that lead into the first of the Canton Lakes (Thunderhead Lake) — was a little more difficult than our previous carry. To begin with, the starting point was well hidden in a back bay and we noticed the trailhead only when Jamie went to investigate a dilapidated wooden dock next to the obscured portage. Also, a steep incline halfway along and a few downed trees blocking the put-in made the going a little tough. However, once we finished the carry and then paddled through a shallow inlet to reach remote Thunderhead Lake, we quickly realized that the extra effort was worth it. Thunderhead was a perfect example of what was to come — breathtaking scenery and no people.

The next portage (also measuring 400 meters) was almost identical to the previous one. After following an abandoned logging road to the left of the take-out, and then making a right approximately 80 meters along, we had a sharp hill and a few fallen trees to carefully maneuver around before reaching Virginia Lake.

It was the fourth portage heading into James Lake that was the worst overall. It measured a long 1,000 meters, and about a quarter of the way along, the trail split. To the left was a faint path leading to a swampy pond. And to the right, the main portage continued on, straight up a sheer slope.

Matt and Teresa were the first to come to the fork and, thinking that no possible portage would ever lead canoeists up such a incline, they continued left toward the pond. It wasn't until the rest of us had reached the put-in, half an hour later, that we noticed two members of our group were missing. It was another hour before we had everything, and everyone, camped on James Lake.

To celebrate surviving our first day of hardship, Jamie broke out four cans of lager. It's not a regular custom for Wanapitei, or me for that matter, to carry canned beer along on a canoe trip. However, the Upper Canada Brewing Company happened to be the sponsor for Matt and Teresa's trip. (They answered a web-page questionnaire asking why they would enjoy a week-long canoe trip with famous author Kevin Callan.) So it was only fitting that we took a sample of the product along with us.

I was grateful that neither Matt nor Teresa took the "famous author" part seriously — they were just looking for a free canoe trip. In fact, I distinctly remember the renowned author himself having to carry the darn cans of lager on each and every portage — now how unfair is that?

The rough portages continued the next day, beginning with a very steep 360-meter path connecting the southwest bay of James Lake with Stiles Lake.

Next, a 560-meter trail from the west end of Stiles Lake to a small, unnamed lake, was the worst portage en route. From the take-out, located to

Finally, we reach remote Bob Lake.

the right of a large beaver dam, to about three-quarters of the way along, was relatively easy walking. But at the bottom of the downhill approaching the put-in, the entire path had been flooded over by an operative beaver. For more than 100 meters we had to make our way through a mixture of mud, water and stinking swamp ooze.

Fred chose to go first, finding all the deep areas for the rest of us to try to avoid. Jamie and I then attempted, unsuccessfully, I might add, to balance our way across on a series of rotten logs. Then, Matt and Teresa, having witnessed our performances, resorted to paddling across in their canoe, also without success.

We called it a day after taking on only one more portage (a 20-meter liftover from the west end of the unnamed lake to Bob Lake) and decided to spend the rest of the afternoon exploring the neighboring old-growth forest on the north end of Obabika.

To reach the stand of trees, we paddled south across Bob Lake. Then, after portaging 175 meters into another unnamed lake, we pulled up at the beginning of the 850-meter portage leading into Shish-Kong Lake. Shish-Kong means "lake at the place of the huge rock," and the location was used as a vision quest site by the Teme-Augama Anishnabai people.

The take-out here had to be one of the muddiest in all of Temagami. However, a network of hiking trails, developed by the Friends of Temagami, linked up with the portage halfway along. Not only did the trail system provide an excellent way to tour the Obabika old-growth, but it also meant that we no longer had to continue to portage the heavy canoes.

The trees growing here represent the densest concentration of old-growth red and white pine in Temagami. They range in age from 130 to 300 years, and attain maximum heights of 30 meters and diameters of 75 centimeters. What's more impressive than the trees themselves, however, is what people went through to protect them. In 1989 the most intense battle between loggers and environmentalists was staged here; 370 protesters, including Bob Rae, leader of the opposition (and soon-to-be premier), were arrested in blockades of the controversial Red Squirrel logging road. By 1996 the Ministry of Natural Resources added another 3,520 hectares of protected forest to the already existing Obabika River Provincial Park.

Our third day en route compared little to our remote paddle through the Canton Lakes and especially our visit to the Obabika old-growth forest. Everything was going well at first. We all decided to make it another early day out on Diamond Lake. Even the 1,200-meter portage, taking us from the north end of Bob Lake and into Diamond Lake, ended up an easy carry — once you pass over the logging road you're almost at the put-in. But once we began paddling east across Diamond Lake, our moods quickly changed. A total of thirty-two canoes crowded the lake, and each time we approached a possible campsite we found it either already occupied or so littered with garbage that we wouldn't dare camp on it. Not surprisingly, we also had a youth group warn us about a nuisance bear that had terrorized canoeists camped on Diamond for the last three weeks. (The bear was eventually shot after it rummaged through food packs on both the island campsites and the neighboring portages one time too many.)

Wanting desperately to escape the mobs gathering on Diamond Lake, and especially to avoid a possible encounter with a problem bear, we continued on to the southeast bay. Here a 75-meter portage, marked on the left of an old sluiceway, took us into Temagami's Sharp Rock Inlet, and by paddling through the northern inlet we chose an out-of-the-way site at the bottom end of Whitefish Bay.

We were lucky to have moved on. Dark clouds hung low over camp the next morning, and halfway through breakfast it began to rain. It would have been a miserable paddle if we had stayed on Diamond. From our site on Whitefish Bay, however, we had only to paddle to the opposite shore to take on the 825-meter Napoleon Portage and then cross Ferguson Bay to reach Wanapitei Lodge.

Even then, the notoriously steep portage was a chore, and by the time we reached Ferguson Bay the rain was pelting down hard and a strong wind was building deep swells out on the lake. It was odd, though, that the closer the group got to the end of the trip, the slower everyone seemed to paddle. No one seemed to want our time out here to end. The clients even asked to stop for lunch, choosing to eat soggy sandwiches out in the pouring rain rather than head for the comfort and safety of the lodge. Jamie and I were dumbfounded. Never had we witnessed a group so distressed about ending a trip. It was a compliment — though not to our guiding abilities, but to the land itself and the ancient Nastawgan that took them there.

TEMAGAMI'S CANTON LAKES

TIME 4–5 days

NUMBER OF PORTAGES 10

LONGEST PORTAGE 1,200 meters

DIFFICULTY Intermediate canoe-tripping skills are required.

ALTERNATIVE ACCESS The Temagami docks, or at the end of the Lake Temagami Access Road (Mine Road).

ALTERNATIVE ROUTE To avoid the rough ride along the Red Squirrel Road, you can begin the route at the town docks or at the end of Lake Temagami Access Road and link up with Sharp Rock Inlet by way of Lake Temagami's North Arm.

OUTFITTERS

WANAPITEI CANOE INC.
Sandy Inlet
Temagami, Ontario
P0H 2H0
705-237-8677
(Summer)

338 Caves Road
R.R. 2, Warsaw, Ontario
K0L 3A0
Toll-free: 1-888-781-0411
705-652-9461
(Winter)

SMOOTHWATER OUTDOOR CENTRE
Box 40, Temagami, Ontario
P0H 2H0
705-569-3539

TEMAGAMI WILDERNESS CENTRE LIMITED
R.R. 1, Temagami, Ontario
P0H 2H0
705-569-3733

TEMAGAMI CANOE OUTFITTING COMPANY
Box 27, Temagami, Ontario
P0H 2H0
705-569-2790

FOR MORE INFORMATION

FRIENDS OF TEMAGAMI
Box 398. Temagami, Ontario
P0H 2H0
705-569-3539 or 705-569-3777
e-mail: temagami@onlink.net
www.smoothwater.com

MINISTRY OF NATURAL RESOURCES
3301 Trout Lake Rd.
North Bay, Ontario
P1A 4L7
705-475-5550

TOPOGRAPHIC MAPS

41 P/1

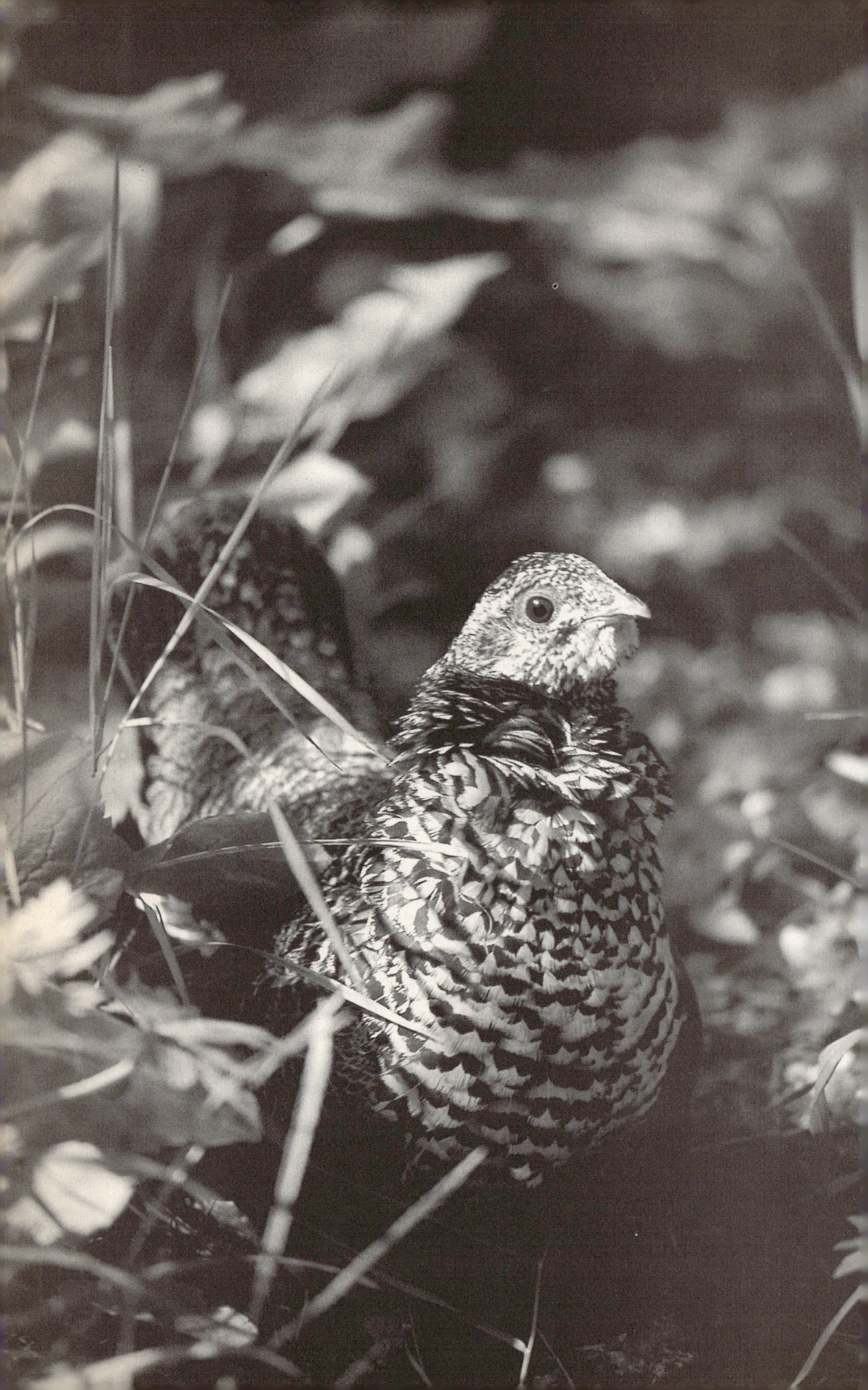

MARTEN RIVER
PROVINCIAL PARK

ACROSS NORTHERN ONTARIO THERE ARE A NUMBER of underused provincial parks that provide direct access to some excellent quick and easy canoe routes. Shoals Provincial Park has a short loop that's perfect for the angler looking for some pike and walleye action. Halfway Lake Provincial Park provides a chain of scenic lakes specifically designed for canoeists. And Obatanga Provincial Park hosts innumerable daytrip and multi-night adventures. But my favorite of these little-known novice routes has to be Marten River Provincial Park. Not only can you easily link up with the extensive Temagami canoe-route system to the west, but to the east there's a lesser known area, the Nipissing Crown Game Reserve, that's just as rewarding.

Marten River Provincial Park promotes two main routes: the Marian Lake Loop and the Marten River Loop. The Marian Lake Loop is the shorter of the two trips but is quickly disappearing due to lack of proper maintenance. Even the Marten River Loop has a lengthy 2,250-meter portage, connecting Wicksteed and Bruce Lakes, that has been so flooded over because of beaver dams it's next to impossible to locate at times. If I had to choose between the two, though, I would go with the second option. Except rather than attempt the portage in between the two main lakes, I would simply paddle to either Wicksteed or Bruce Lake and then return via the same route.

Only a quick paddle across Little Marten and Big Marten Lakes is necessary to reach Bruce Lake, with no portages in between. But I prefer Wicksteed Lake. It's connected to Little Marten Lake by a 175-meter portage (marked to the right of a concrete dam). But it also has the advantage of more

Giving a spruce grouse the right-of-way along the overgrown portage between Wicksteed and Bruce Lakes.

140 ONTARIO'S LOST CANOE ROUTES

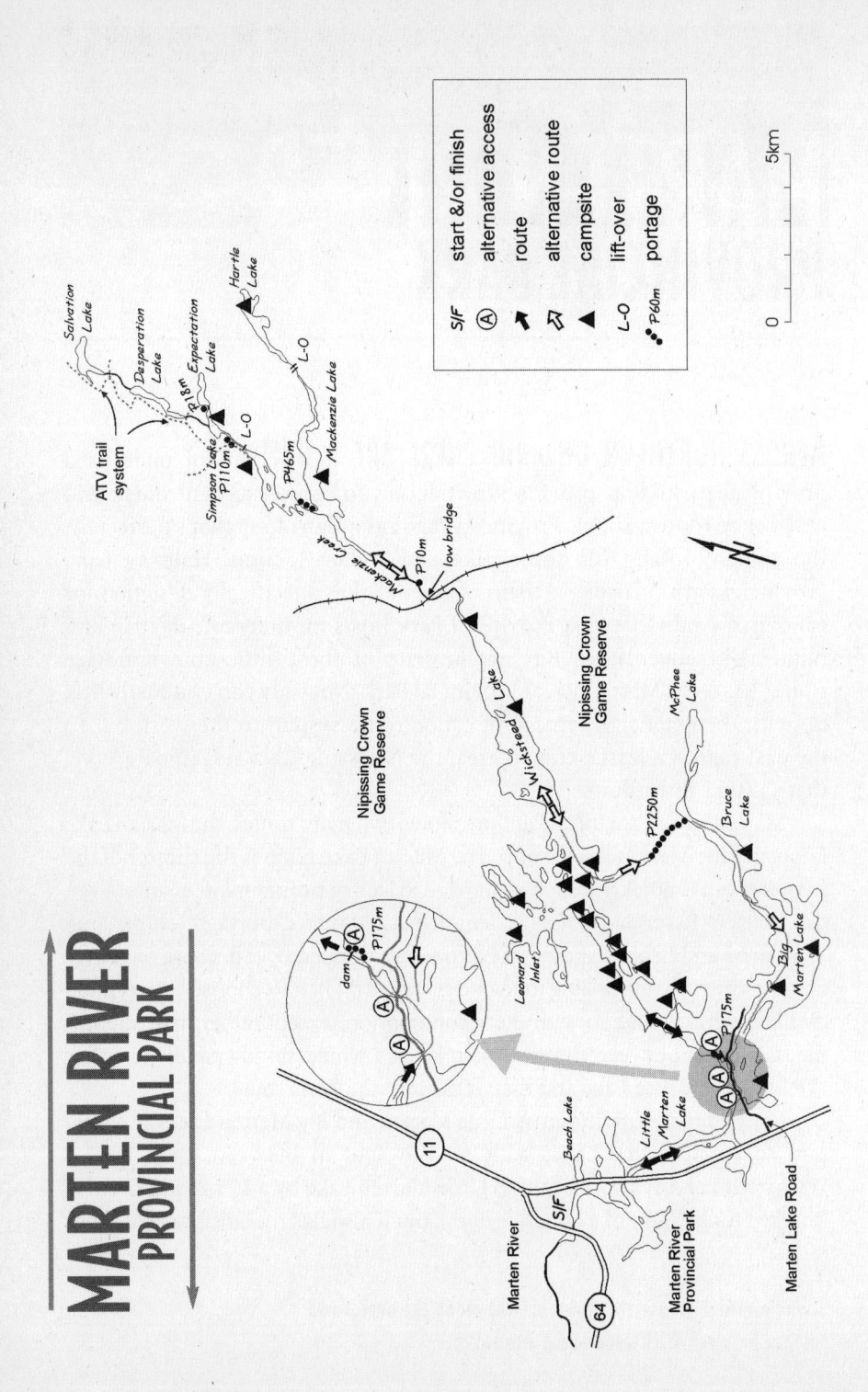

A quite morning on the north shore of Wicksteed Lake.

campsites and much better fishing, not to mention a government boat launch at its south end, beside the concrete dam. The launch is handy if you happen to arrive late in the day and don't have time to paddle the 8 kilometers out from the provincial park.

To reach the alternative put-in, drive 6 kilometers south of Marten River Provincial Park, on Highway 11, and then turn east on to Marten Lake Road. From here, drive another 2.8 kilometers and then veer left onto a bumpier road leading down to the launching area beside the dam.

If you're worried about your vehicle on the last bit of rough road, you also have the option of parking alongside one of the two Bailey bridges, just before the turnoff. From here you have only to paddle up a shallow channel to reach the launch area, and then make use of the 175-meter portage to the right of the dam.

At first the lake is quite narrow and will probably be overrun with motorboats, especially if you choose a long weekend to venture out. Once you have reached the halfway mark, however, the lake spreads out and the numerous islands, bays and inlets help relieve most of the heavy boat traffic.

The prime campsites are found along the east shoreline, 3 kilometers up from the boat launch, as well as on the center islands, 6 kilometers across the lake. Canoeists looking for a more secluded spot, however, are best to head west into Leonard Inlet or behind the islands along the east shore.

Loons cruising by the campsite to gawk at the new neighbors (Salvation Lake).

Wicksteed Lake is quite large. With its numerous bays and inlets, all bordered by monstrous pine trees, you could spend an entire weekend just exploring the lake itself. For the more adventurous, however, there's a side route to MacKenzie Lake and Simpson Lake, accessible from the top end of Wicksteed via MacKenzie Creek. You'll have to cross only a short 10-meter portage, on the right of MacKenzie Creek, approximately half a kilometer past the rail bridge, and a 465-meter portage connecting the western inlet of MacKenzie Lake to the south end of Simpson Lake.

If you continue north out of Simpson Lake by way of MacKenzie Creek you can also explore three smaller lakes — Expectation Lake, Desperation Lake and Salvation Lake. The names are intriguing. According to a local trapper, Bob Groves, they come from the story of a Native family. The family had planned to rendezvous at Expectation Lake and had arrived low on provisions. Moving into Desperation Lake, times were getting a little harder, but they finally met up with people and supplies at Salvation Lake. But the 110-meter portage on the left of the creek linking Expectation Lake with Simpson Lake is fairly grown-over and the trails in between to Desperation and Salvation Lake are almost completely non-existent. All of these things make a restful stay on Wicksteed a far better option.

MARTEN RIVER PROVINCIAL PARK

TIME 2–3 days

NUMBER OF PORTAGES 2

LONGEST PORTAGE 175 meters

DIFFICULTY This is considered a novice canoe route.

ALTERNATIVE ACCESS You can reach the public boat launch on Wicksteed Lake by driving 6 kilometers south of Marten River Provincial Park, on Highway 11, and then turning east on to Marten Lake Road. From here, drive another 2.8 kilometers and then veer left onto a bumpier road leading down to the launching area beside the dam. If you're worried about the rough road, you also have the option of parking alongside one of the two Bailey bridges, just before the turnoff.

ALTERNATIVE ROUTE Take a side trip from the northeast of Wicksteed Lake into MacKenzie Lake and Simpson Lake, via MacKenzie Creek.

OUTFITTERS

DOUGALL'S GUIDING SERVICE & ACCOMMODATIONS
General Delivery
Marten River, Ontario
P0H 1T0
705-892-2207

SMOOTHWATER OUTDOOR CENTRE
Box 40
Temagami, Ontario
P0H 2H0
705-569-3539

TEMAGAMI WILDERNESS CENTRE LIMITED
R.R. 1
Temagami, Ontario
P0H 2H0
705-569-3733

TEMAGAMI CANOE OUTFITTING COMPANY
Box 27
Temagami, Ontario
P0H 2H0
705-569-2790

FOR MORE INFORMATION

MARTEN RIVER PROVINCIAL PARK
General Delivery
Marten River, Ontario
P0H 1T0
705-892-2200

TOPOGRAPHIC MAPS
31 L/12 & 31 L/13

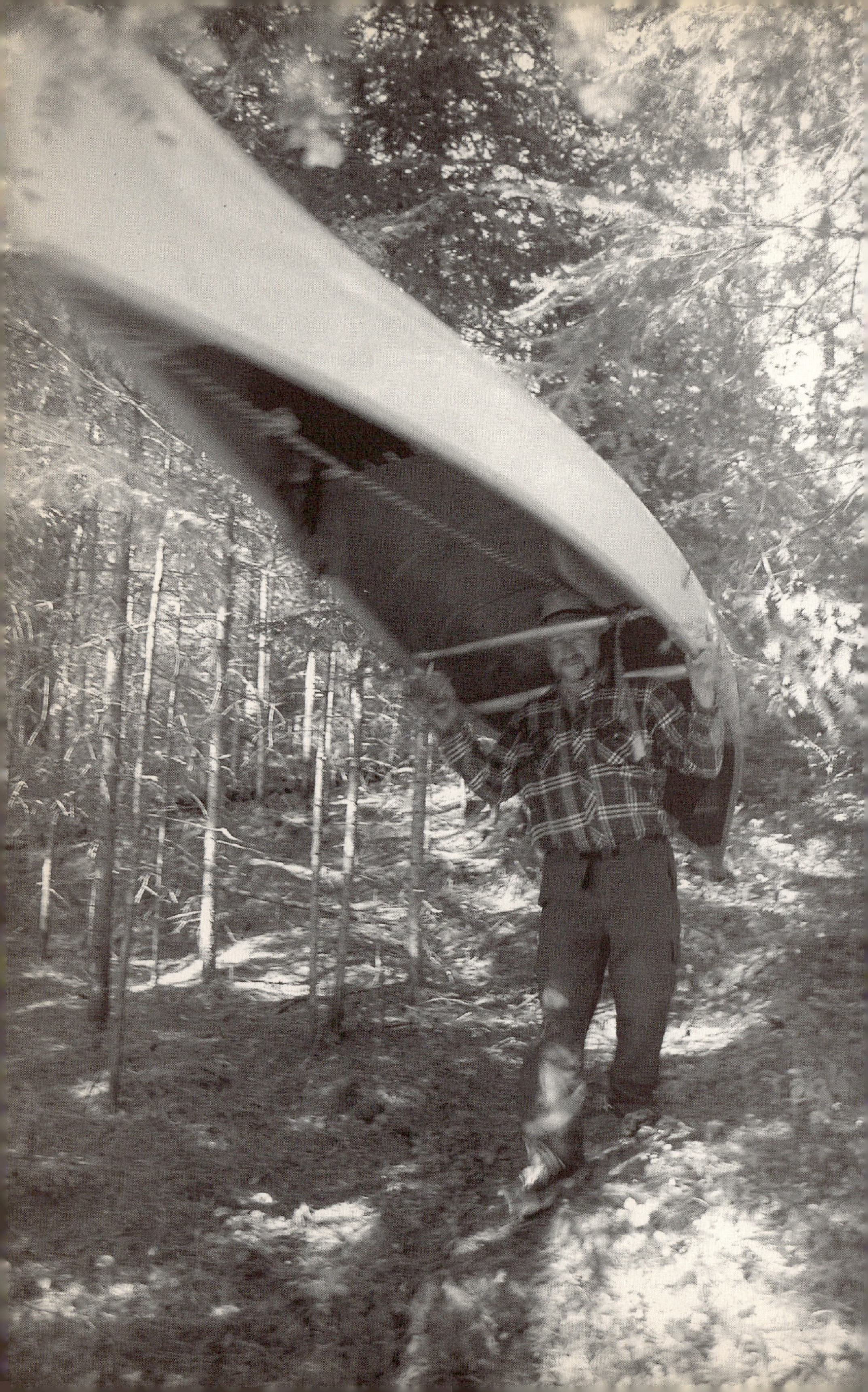

SOUTH RIVER

JUST AS THE OXTONGUE RIVER was used as the main access to Algonquin Provincial Park before the 1930s, the South River was the primary exit. As far back as 1903, outdoor writer James Edmund Jones, while including suggested canoe trips in his book *Canoeing and Camping*, added a chapter "From Dwight to South River." Then, in 1915, painter Tom Thomson ended his first extensive trip through Algonquin by way of the South River (where along the way he supposedly met up with the legendary Grey Owl and cooked him doughnuts). And in 1926, when Camp Pathfinder began extending their canoe outings further afield, the South River train station quickly became a way for the youth camp to get back to their home base at the bottom end of the park.

Throughout the years, however, Algonquin gained a number of easier take-out points and canoeists quickly abandoned the South River route — until recently, that is. In the spring of 2000, Terry Graham, owner of Canadian Wilderness Trips, re-cut a series of portages once used to link Kawawaymog Lake with the river itself. The next season, after hearing about his work on the historic route, I headed up to give it a try.

Originally, my intention was to retrace that exact route by beginning from Terry's base camp on the west shore of Kawawaymog Lake, portaging through the "rediscovered" trails, and then paddling down to the town by the lower half of the South River. Not necessarily wanting to organize a car shuttle, I decided on a possible circle route instead. From Kawawaymog I would head east into Algonquin Provincial Park and then loop back by making use of a series of small lakes and the upper section of the South River, then reconnect with Kawawaymog Lake by traveling north on the old portages.

It's Hugh's turn to carry the canoe, on the portage between Maryjane Lake and Kawawaymog Lake.

146 ONTARIO'S LOST CANOE ROUTES

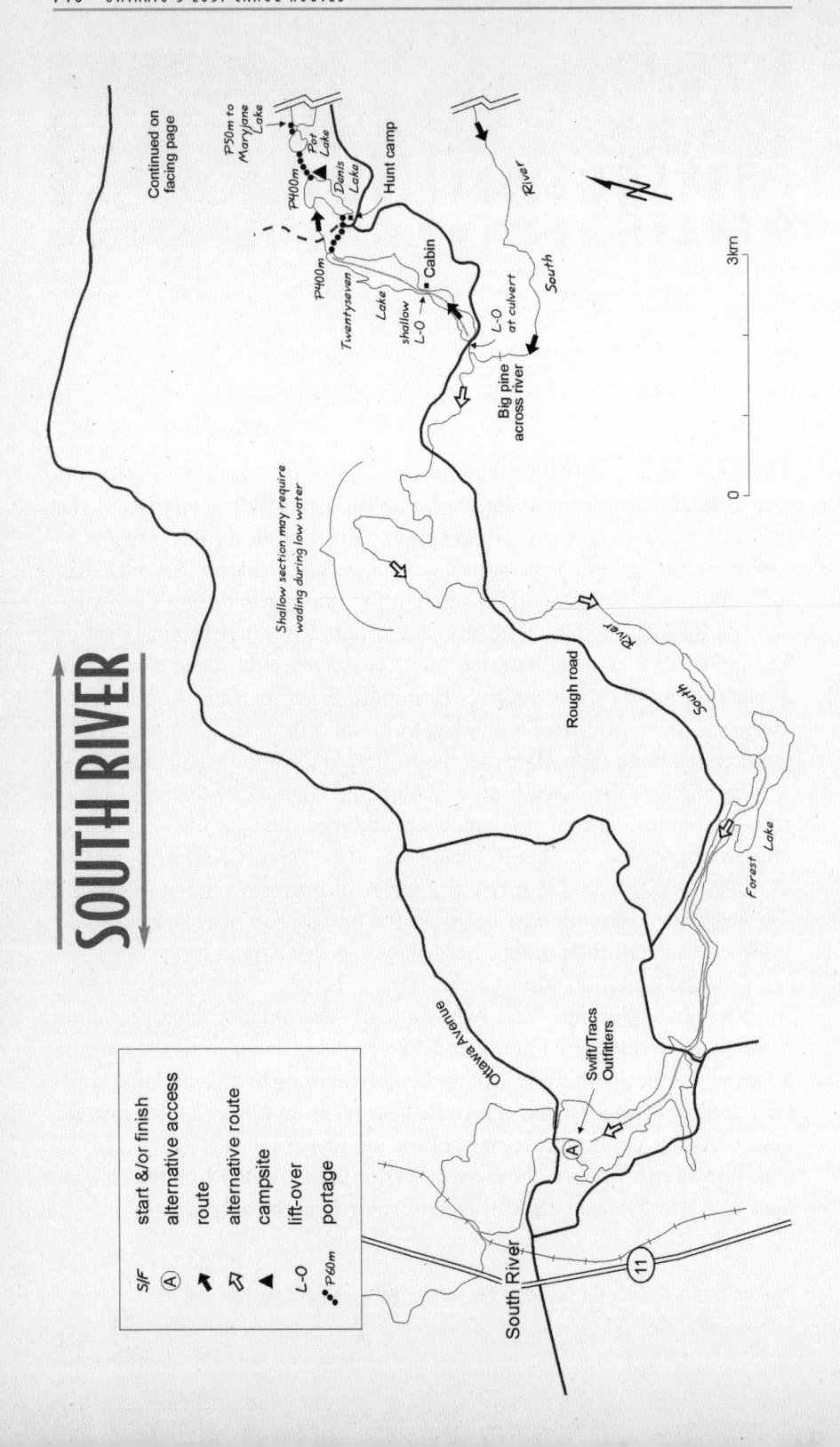

SOUTH RIVER

Continued on facing page

P50m to Maryjane Lake
Pot Lake
Denis Lake
P400m
Hunt camp
P400m
Twentyseven Lake
shallow L-O
Cabin
L-O at culvert
Big pine across river
South River

Shallow section may require wading during low water

Rough road

South River

Forest Lake

Ottawa Avenue

Swift/Tracs Outfitters

(A)

South River

11

0   3km
N

Legend:
- S/F — start &/or finish
- (A) — alternative access
- → — route
- ⇨ — alternative route
- ▲ — campsite
- L-O — lift-over
- P60m — portage

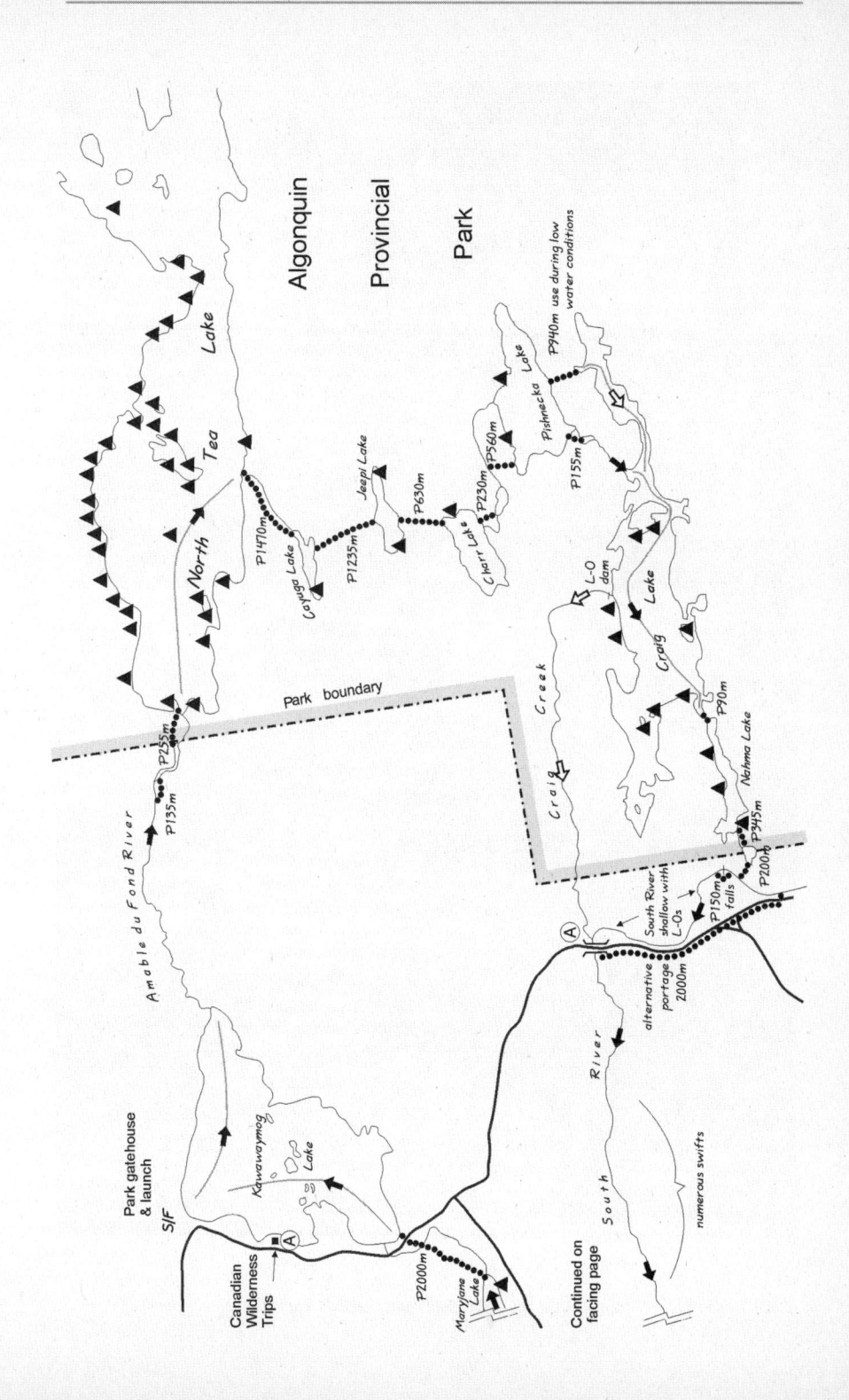

SOUTH RIVER 147

Boris boils up afternoon tea on his homemade one-burner woodstove.

Agreeing to join me on the trip was canoe mate Hugh Banks, a fellow instructor at Sir Sanford Fleming College, and Boris Swidersky, editor of *Bushwacker* magazine. Hugh had already accompanied me on a number of exploratory routes, and Boris was looking for more content for his "off-trail" periodical, so we made a perfect team. Thus on the first Saturday in June, when water levels were high and the bug population was even higher, we headed off for the unknown.

To reach the Kawawaymog access point, located just outside Algonquin's western border, we turned east off Highway 11 onto Ottawa Avenue, in South River. A 22-kilometer drive down a gravel road led us to the park gatehouse, where we picked up our permit for the two nights we would need to stay in the park.

The usual put-in is directly beside the gatehouse. We all agreed, however, that Terry's camp, situated only a couple more kilometers down the road, would make a better place to begin and end our trip.

From the camp we paddled east, passing the same cluster of islands where painter Tom Thomson used to spend time looking over his work — including *Chill November, Sand Hill* and *The West Wind* — after returning from one of his sketching trips in the park. Notably, he would spread out his work, keeping only a few paintings, and then give what remained to his friend and park ranger, Tom Wattie, to either keep or burn. (Wattie later remarked that the sketch boards made a brilliantly colored bonfire.)

From the islands we headed to the Amble du Fond River, located on the far northeast corner of Kawawaymog Lake. The river, which marks the entrance into Algonquin Provincial Park, meanders uncontrollably for more than 4 kilometers and has two portages (a 135 meter to the right and a 255 meter to the left) near the entrance to North Tea Lake. With a strong east wind blowing across North Tea, it was midday before we found ourselves at the take-out for the portage (1,470 meters) leading into Cayuga Lake.

After dealing with the heavy winds on North Tea, we were glad to be on dry land — until the bugs found us. A good mixture of blackflies and mosquitoes attacked by the thousands. Instantly we took to the portage, only to find more bugs waiting for us on the trail. And what a trail it was. The long distance was challenging enough. But a steep hill near the take-out and four mud-filled creek crossings were added on for good measure. The portage took almost two hours to complete and it was 7 p.m. by the time we paddled out into Cayuga Lake.

Our initial plan was to camp on Jeepi Lake, which is connected to Cayuga Lake by a lengthy 1,235-meter portage. Since it was so late, however, we made the group decision to break park rules (you must stay on the designated lake stated on your permit) and stop on Cayuga. The three of us weren't too concerned about camping illegally, since there was little chance for another group to arrive on the lake that night. What did bother us, however, was that we were already behind schedule and were becoming completely exhausted and we hadn't even reached the unmaintained section of the route.

To help keep to our agenda we packed up and headed for the Jeepi Lake portage at dawn. The 1,235-meter trail was far worse than the previous portage into Cayuga. It had no muddy creeks to step across but the bug's population had doubled along the trail and a total of four steep inclines made the carry an exhausting ordeal.

Sadly, only a five-minute paddle across Jeepi Lake brought us to another lengthy portage, this time along a 630-meter trail to Charr Lake. It was somewhat easier, though, with only one hill halfway along. And the next portage, 230 meters long and marked to the left of where a creek flows into Charr Lake, was completely flat.

Then, after a short paddle up a marshy stream, we negotiated another relatively flat and easy 560-meter portage (marked to the right of where the waterway begins to open up) into Pishnecka Lake.

Obviously, things were looking up. To end our second day, we had only to carry over into Craig Lake. There were two options: paddle southeast across Pishnecka Lake and follow a 940-meter portage up and over a steep knoll, or keep to the right-hand shoreline and portage only 155 meters to where a shallow creek leads into Craig Lake. The difficult 940-meter portage was used when the creek was unnavigable due to low water. Luckily a heavy rainstorm the night before had kept water levels high and we were able to paddle down the stream quite easily.

By 2 p.m. Hugh, Boris and I found ourselves relaxing on a prime campsite, adjacent to the Craig Lake dam.

In hindsight, we should have continued on for at least another hour or so. Our park permit was for Craig Lake, though. The dam also marked the spot where we had to choose our route to the South River, either portaging around the dam to Craig Creek or paddling east across Craig and Nahma Lakes.

Terry had suggested Craig Creek. He had never been on the upper section of the South River, between Nahma Lake and the confluence of Craig Creek itself, but thought it might be too shallow. Craig Creek also had a number of gravel swifts that would make things interesting, as long as the dam was kept open, of course. But as luck would have it, the dam was closed shut when we arrived.

It was a tough choice: a dried-up creek bed or an unknown section of river that might also be dried up. But the South River was not dam controlled, and so because of the constant rain we had received during the previous couple of days, we opted for the secondary route.

Anxious about what lay ahead, we were again up early, looking for the portage into Nahma Lake. The 90-meter trail was located to the southwest on Craig, tucked out of the way in a small lagoon.

From here we paddled across Nahma Lake and made two more consecutive portages (345 meters and 200 meters) in and out of a small pond.

At the put-in of the last portage we finally met up with the South River. Here again, we had two choices: paddle upstream to begin portaging north along a dirt road for over 2 kilometers or head downstream and hope for an easy ride down to the confluence of the South River and Craig Creek.

After deliberating over a midmorning snack of jujubes and GORP, we decided on the downstream run. Seconds later, we were halted by a double cascade. The waterfall wasn't a complete surprise to us, since the topo map did indicate some drop in elevation here. It was the idea of pushing our way through the overgrown portage marked on the left that made us rethink our decision. It was only 150 meters long, but there were enough trees fallen across it that we wondered if we would ever get to the other side

Not wanting to portage along a lengthy road, however, we kept with the river route. It took us a good half-hour to drag everything through the insignificant trail, but things went quite smoothly after that. The downstream run, from the falls to the confluence of Craig Creek, was small but navigable with only a couple of fallen trees to lift over, a few swifts to maneuver through, and some tight spots where alders grew thick along the bank. Mind you, it would've been a totally different story if water levels had been down.

Once we passed under a bridge, not far downstream from where Craig Creek flushes in from the east, the river widened its banks considerably. The quick current remained, however, and for a good 5 kilometers we enjoyed countless swifts. It was an impressive run. Even the sections between rapids were pretty and serene, the current continuing to hurry along, but without real effort, past massive pine left over from the logging days.

The lumbermen cut the prime white pine mostly off Trout Creek and the South River flats about 1889 and drove them down to Lake Nipissing each spring. The best quality trees were made into square timber, while many lesser quality pine were left untouched. These are the ones that remain along the banks, and they're magnificent.

Limbo contestants Hugh and Boris make their way under a logjam on the South River.

A number of rock sluiceways were also noticeable along the way, which allowed our group to maneuver down most of the shallow sections of the river without getting our feet wet. Originally the small rock-piles were constructed by the men working for 19th-century lumber baron J. R. Booth; park wardens patrolling the river for poachers continued to maintain them until the early to mid-1900s.

The current eventually slowed down around the halfway mark, and we soon came upon a few logjams that had to be lifted over as we continued downriver. Eventually, by 3:30 p.m., we reached where the route headed north. Here, after pulling over a giant pine log, we paddled for another fifteen minutes and then turned right, entering a side channel leading to a metal culvert placed under a dirt road. This ended our trip on the South River and marked the beginning of our journey along the historic portages leading back to Kawawaymog Lake.

We had to get out and wade here and, rather than portage directly over the road, decided to simply walk straight through the culvert. From here we entered the south bay of Twentyseven Lake. The lake, locally and appropriately known as Clear Lake, is divided into two sections by a shallow creek. There was barely enough water to paddle through at the time, so once again we had to get out and wade.

It was a little unnerving to be out of the canoe here. Rumor had it that the owner of the cabin on the north end absolutely detested anyone coming so close to his property. He even had a homemade potato gun resting on top of an old cannon mount, pointing directly at the creek. Lucky for us, however, there was no one on guard while we passed through, and after quickly wading by, we made haste up the lake.

It was our plan that day to make camp on the top end of Twentyseven Lake rather than clear a bush site along the South River. As it happened, the river would have been a better choice. There was no designated campsite anywhere on the lake — not even a bit of flat shoreline big enough for a single tent.

The decision was then made to continue on to Denis Lake (formerly Henry Lake) — our second bad resolution of the day. First, the take-out of the 400-meter trail, located on the northeast corner of Twentyseven Lake, was less than obvious. The put-in was also out of sight, up a dirt road to the right and behind a hunt camp. After all that, it was quite late by the time we started searching the shoreline for any possible place to camp. By 7 p.m. we found ourselves set up on a clearing on the far end of the lake. There was no firepit or tent pad, just an open area back in the bush that had been used the previous winter by a local dogsled company. We did our best to practice low-impact camping, making it difficult to even notice that we had ever stayed there.

We were up early the next morning, desperately searching for the whereabouts of the second "lost" portage, a 400-meter trail leading into Pot Lake. Terry, the outfitter back on Kawawaymog Lake, had told us that we first had to walk across a wet, grassy area at the far east end of Denis Lake before reaching the take-out. The three of us scattered ourselves along the shoreline and spent half an hour searching. But it wasn't until Boris wandered back toward our campsite, at the extreme corner of the marsh, that he noticed the faint path leading into the woods.

From Pot Lake to Maryjane Lake there was only a quick 50-meter portage to the left of a creek. However, the next portage, from Maryjane Lake back to the familiar Kawawaymog Lake, also found to the left of another creek, was a complete nightmare. A makeshift portage sign, the first we had noticed outside the park, was the only positive thing about the extensive

2,000-meter trail. The first quarter was plagued by steep hills and the last quarter cursed with boot-sucking mud. And in between was an indefinite path blocked with fallen trees and obscured by various side trails. On the first trip over, Boris, who was in the lead, had to pull out his compass four times to confirm that we were at least traveling in the right direction.

It took us two hours to carry everything over to where a road cuts across the portage (the trail picks up again 20 meters to the right for the final 200 meters). In hindsight, we should have paid more attention to James Edmund Jones's 1903 guide. He suggested back then that canoeists should obtain a wagon and take the tote road from Clear Lake (Twentyseven Lake) to Round Lake (Kawawaymog Lake). Even Tom Thomson cheated at times by hitching a ride back on the neighboring log-train operated by the Standard Chemical Company in the town of South River.

But then again, if we'd avoided the series of lakes between Kawawaymog Lake and the South River we would have missed out on some incredible scenery. We also would never have spotted an osprey nest on Denis Lake or Maryjane Lake or watched a family of otter swimming across Pot Lake. And the sight of the impressive old-growth rooted alongside the portages, especially rare stands of maple and yellow birch, was well worth our efforts. Better yet, we were all able to step back in time for a while, to travel a route that was once a regular thoroughfare and is now left in complete obscurity — which is something all canoeists would agree is a rarity in this day and age.

SOUTH RIVER

TIME 2–3 days

NUMBER OF PORTAGES 16

LONGEST PORTAGE 2,000 meters

DIFFICULTY

No experience is required running rapids but at least intermediate skills are necessary because the route is physically demanding. The alternative route is rated as a novice trip, however.

ALTERNATIVE ACCESS You can use the parking area on the northwest side of the South River bridge, which is reached by continuing a few kilometers past the access at

Kawawaymog Lake. Swift Canoe in South River can also be used as an alternative take-out.

ALTERNATIVE ROUTE The South River itself makes an exceptional daytrip during high water levels, especially from the South River bridge, just east of Algonquin's border, to the town of South River (you need at least six hours to complete the entire paddle). Swift Canoe, located on the east end of town, makes the best take-out.

OUTFITTERS

CANADIAN WILDERNESS TRIP
45 Charles St. E., Suite 100
Toronto, Ontario
M4Y 1S2
416-960-2298
e-mail: cwt@inforamp.net
www.CdnWildernessTrips.com

NORTHERN EDGE ALGONQUIN
Box 329
South River, Ontario
P0A 1X0
Toll-free: 800-953-3343
or 705-386-1595
e-mail: edge@algonquincanada.com
www.algonquincanada.com

NORTHERN WILDERNESS OUTFITTERS
Box 89
South River, Ontario
P0A 1X0

Toll-free: 705-474-3272
or 705-386-0466
e-mail: now@efni.com
www.northernwilderness.com

VOYAGEUR OUTFITTING
Box 67055
Toronto, Ontario
M4P 3C8
Toll-free: 877-837-8889
e-mail: dmacvoy@ican.net
home.ican.net/~macvoy

SWIFT/TRACS OUTFITTERS
South River, Ontario
P0A 1X0
705-386-1564
e-mail: tracs@tracsoutfitter.com
www.swiftcanoe.com

FOR MORE INFORMATION

ALGONQUIN PROVINCIAL PARK
Box 219
Whitney, Ontario
K0J 2M0
705-633-5572
1-888-668-7275 (reservations)

TOPOGRAPHIC MAPS

31 E/14

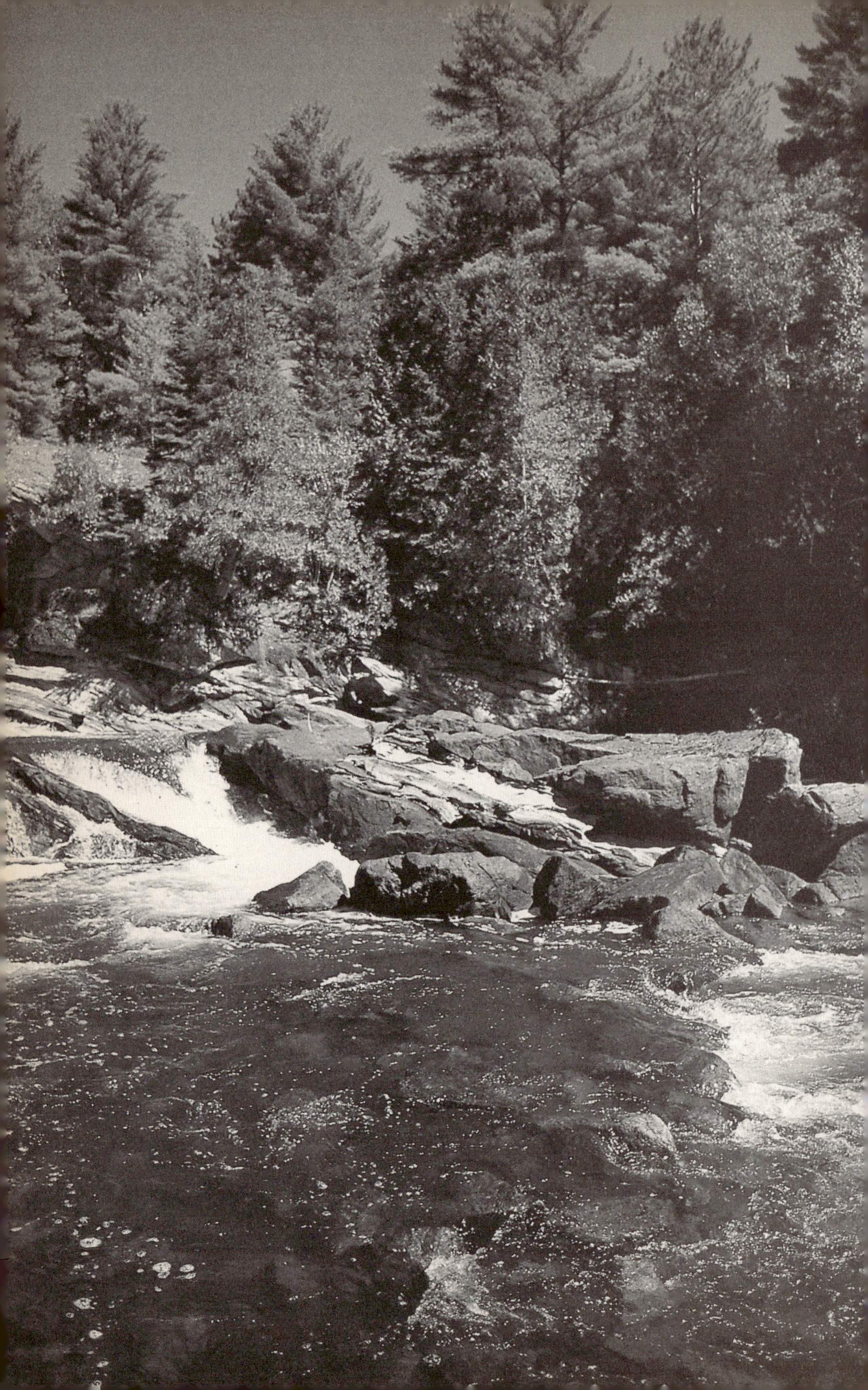

YORK RIVER

For countless years the York River was used as a major waterway. Algonquin tribes used it while retreating from the invading Iroquois. Fur traders used it as part of a transport route from Georgian Bay to the Ottawa River. Lumber companies based in Haliburton began flushing their logs down it before making use of any other neighboring tributary. Even the initial surveyors remarked it was a great-grandchild of the mighty St. Lawrence. But for a while now it's basically been forgotten. In fact, I can't recall ever seeing another canoeist while on the river. And for that reason alone, it definitely fits the "lost canoe route" category.

The best section of the river to paddle is between Egan Chutes Provincial Park and Conroy Marsh. It's a perfect two-day outing for novice canoeists or advanced paddlers looking for a leisurely getaway.

Egan Chutes Provincial Park is 11 kilometers east of Bancroft, along Highway 28; the public access road is northeast of the highway bridge. Take note, however, that the park is no longer regularly maintained by the province and has only a small clearing below the remains of an old concrete dam acting as the put-in site. Also, since it's a river route, you'll have to shuttle a second vehicle to the public launch at the west end of Combermere, along Highway 62.

Not far from the starting point is Egan Chute itself, named after Lumber Baron John Egan, who, in the mid-1800s, built a number of timber chutes along the York River. He was in fact one of the first to hold a timber license in the district (1847), driving most of his logs down the river from nearby Baptiste Lake.

Farm Chute, York River.

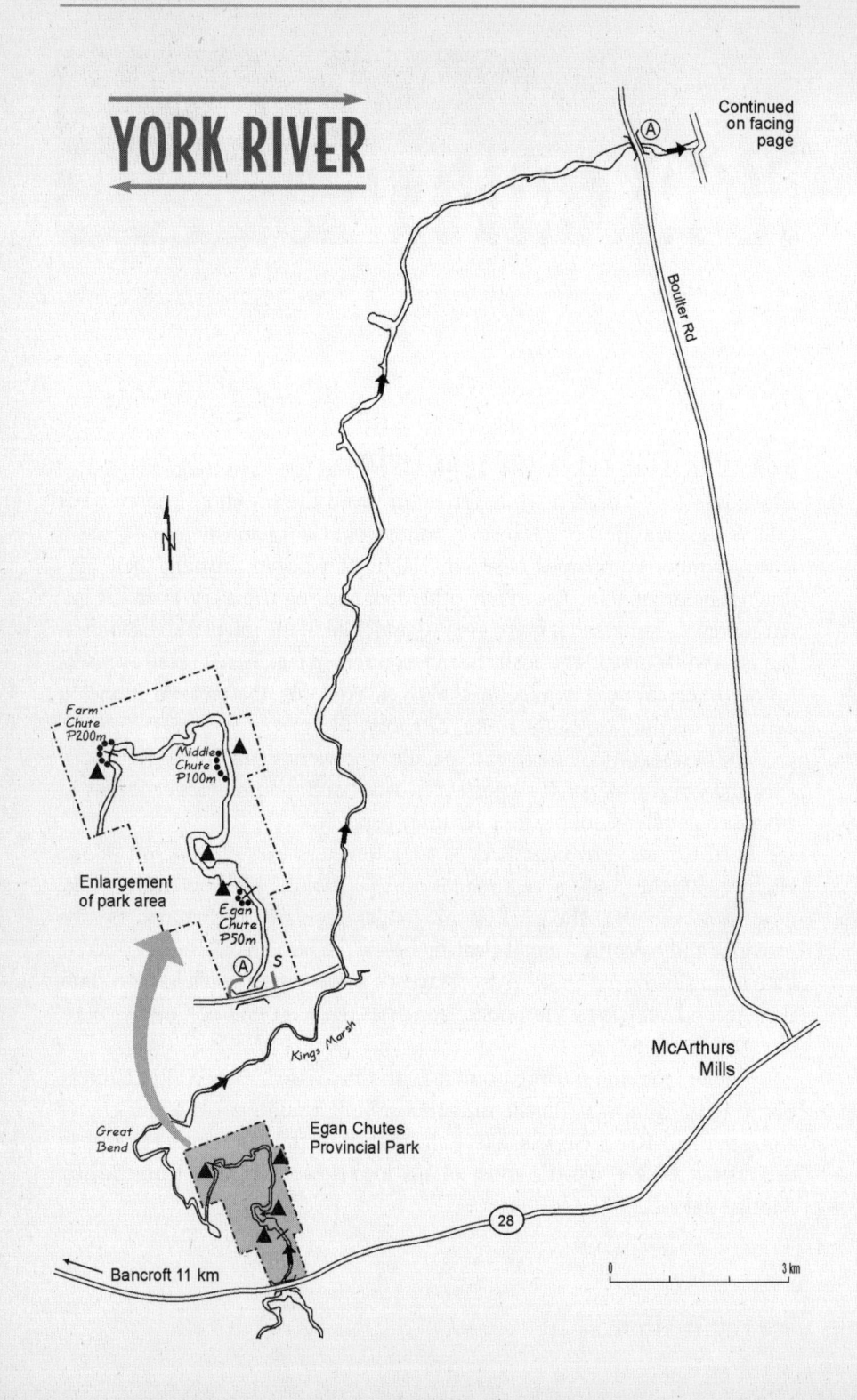

YORK RIVER

Map content:

- Continued on facing page
- Boulter Rd
- Farm Chute P200m
- Middle Chute P100m
- Egan Chute P50m
- Enlargement of park area
- King's Marsh
- McArthurs Mills
- Great Bend
- Egan Chutes Provincial Park
- Bancroft 11 km
- 28
- 0 — 3 km

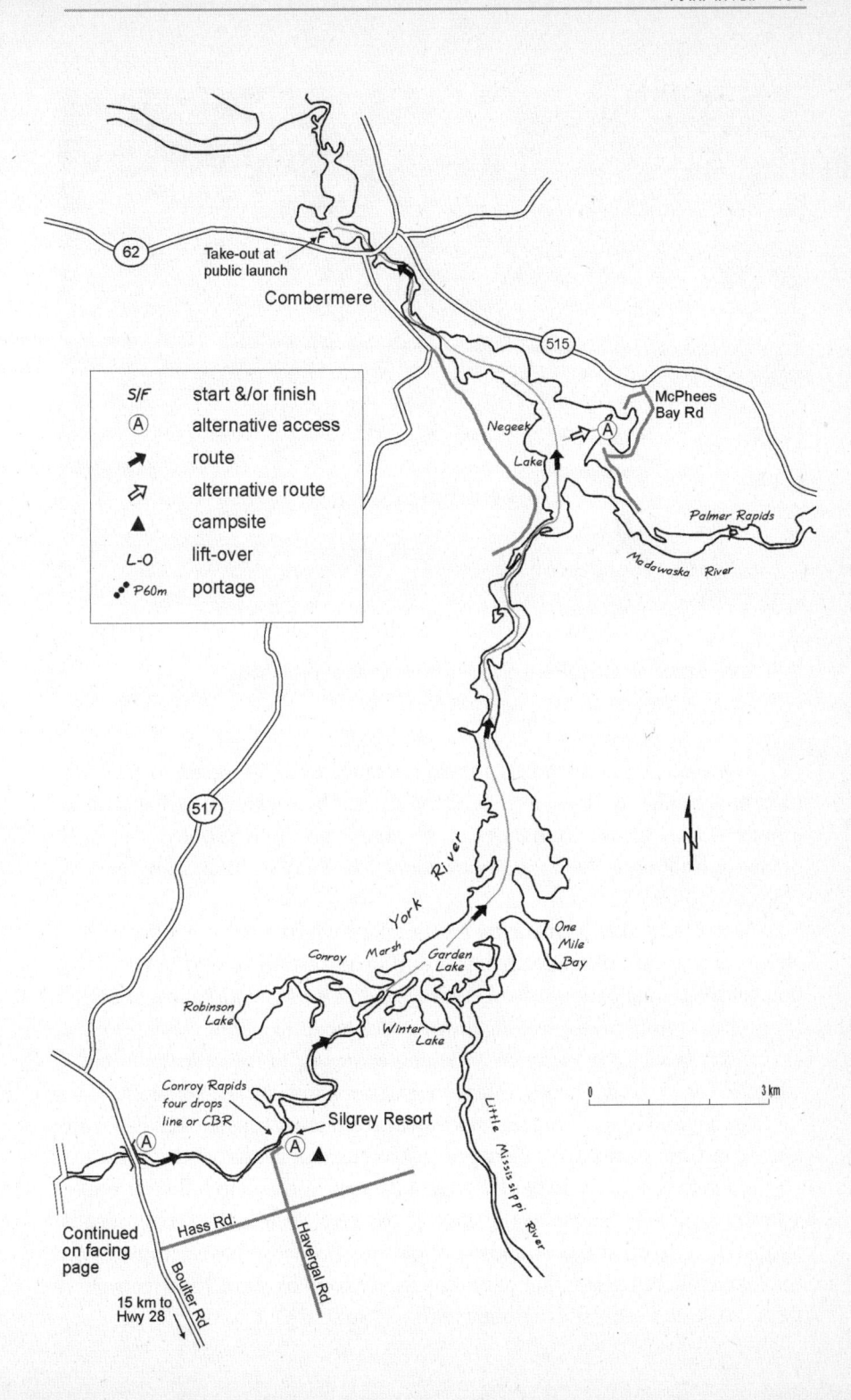

YORK RIVER 159

Bailey dries herself off after almost plunging to her death at Egan Chute.

To the left of the cascade is a short but fairly steep 50-meter portage. It's used on a regular basis — not by canoeists, but by rockhounds. Bancroft is known as the Mineral Capital of Canada, and Egan Chute is one of the local hotspots, holding a high quantity of nepheline, sodalite, biotite, zircon, and blue corundum.

Egan Chute also happens to be the place where my poor dog, Bailey, almost plummeted to her death. It was during my last trip down the York. The dog, for some unapparent reason, decided to go for a swim just above the falls. In seconds I found myself leaping down a rock face and grabbing her paw just as she was going over the brink. The dog came out of the ordeal without a scratch. I, on the other hand, suffered a split knee and cracked shinbone.

Just beyond Egan Chute are two more prominent drops — Middle Chute and Farm Chute. Both have portages (100 meters on the left and 200 meters on the right), but these are hardly used and can be difficult to follow at times. The first trail keeps close to the edge of the river, where the second heads almost directly up and over a knob of granite. Both also have campsites on the east bank. But again, they are rarely used except by some local teenagers. (Middle Chute's campsite has been marked "Buzzed Out Point.")

Stands of soft maple dominate the shoreline along the York River, especially between the Great Bend and King's Marsh.

Other sites are found not far downstream, situated on one of the many sandbars found between the Great Bend (where the river takes a dramatic twist to the northeast) and Kings Marsh. I've always arrived at these sites too early in the trip, however, and much prefer to make my own site further downstream — making sure to practice low-impact camping, of course. This stretch, with its large sections of deciduous swamps and forest levees, suits the York's Native name, Shawashkong (the river of marshes), and is my favorite place to paddle along the river.

If you're not that interested in making your own bush camp, it is possible to paddle a full six-to-eight-hour day and end your trip at the alternative take-out at the Boulter Road bridge. Better yet, you could also choose to book a cabin at Silgrey Resort, situated just below the Boulter bridge, on the south side of Conroy Rapids (four sets of swifts that can easily be run or lined down).

However, if you paddle only the first half of the route, you miss the most significant portion — Conroy Marsh — altogether.

This unique wetland, named after Robert Conroy, who held a timber license on land west of Robinson Lake, drained by the York River, was made

Conroy Marsh, one of the largest wetland habitats in Ontario, is an easy place to find yourself lost in.

famous some years ago after Group of Seven member A. J. Casson depicted it on canvas. And because of its richly diverse plant and animal life, as well its beautiful setting in the majestic hills of the Madawaska Highlands, the government soon made it a Crown Game Reserve. Recently, it also was designated a new park under the Living Legacy program.

Because of its size, it's also an easy place to find yourself lost in. A couple of kilometers downstream from Conroy Rapids the waterway spreads out over 2,400 hectares, with Robinson Lake to the west and Winter Lake, Garden Lake, One Mile Bay and the mouth of the Little Mississippi River to the east. To help keep yourself on track, it's best to stay in the center of the main channel and eventually you'll meet up with Negeek Lake, where the York River flushes into the Madawaska River.

From here it's just a short paddle west, under the Highway 62 bridge, and then left toward the public launch in Combermere. Or, if you don't happen to have a not-so-bright dog prone to swimming above waterfalls, you could travel east on the Madawaska and take in a week of adventurous whitewater paddling all the way down to the Ottawa River.

YORK RIVER

TIME 1–2 days

NUMBER OF PORTAGES 3

LONGEST PORTAGE 200 meters

DIFFICULTY The portages around Egan, Middle and Farm Chute are extremely steep but the river itself is still considered a novice route.

ALTERNATIVE ACCESS Put in from the Boulter Road bridge or Silgrey Resort, reached by turning east off Boulter Road onto Hass Road, and then left on Havergal Road. You can also access the river at the end of McPhees Bay Road off Highway 515.

ALTERNATIVE ROUTE The route can be divided into two daytrips by making use of the Boulter Road bridge access or Silgrey Resort.

OUTFITTERS

SILGREY RESORT
General Delivery
Boulter, Ontario
K0L 1G0
613-332-1072
e-mail: silgreyresort@northcom.net

EARTH CONNECTIONS
Box 1646
Bancroft, Ontario
K0L 1C0
1-877-368-8687
613-332-6807
e-mail: earthcon@northcom.net
www.earthcon.on.ca

TOPOGRAPHIC MAPS
31 F/4 & 31 F/5

BIBLIOGRAPHY

Abell, Sam. "Refuge from Civilization." *National Geographic*, Dec. 1978.

Bennet, Doug and Tim Tiner. *Up North: A Guide to Ontario's Wilderness from Blackflies to Northern Lights*. Canada: Reed Books, 1993.

Brunton, Daniel. "Woodland Caribou." *Seasons*. Toronto: Federation of Ontario Naturalists, summer 1986.

Carpenter, Donna. *A Camper's Guide to Ontario's Best Parks*. Erin: Boston Mills Press, 2000.

Crockman, Joel and Marg. "Perceptions of a Wildland Winter." *Seasons*, Toronto: Federation of Ontario Naturalists, summer 1981.

Crossing the High Portage: A Guide to the Gogama Area. Gogama Chamber of Commerce. Gogama, Ont.: 2000.

Cummings, Dr. "Caribou Country." *Seasons*, Toronto: Federation of Ontario Naturalists, summer 1981.

Globe and Mail. "Renaissance Man Becoming Northern Legend." Toronto: 1973.

Haig, Don. "Dunlop Lake – Mace Lake Canoe Route." *Nastawagan: The Quarterly Journal of the Wilderness Canoe Association*. Toronto: Wilderness Canoe Association, winter 1999.

Hall, Nancy. "Temagami: The Battle to Protect 'Deep Water' Country." *Borealis*. Toronto: Canadian Parks and Wilderness Association, summer 1990.

Harting, Tony. "Steel River." *Nastawagan: The Quarterly Journal of the Wilderness Canoe Association*. Toronto: Wilderness Canoe Association, autumn 1992.

Hodgins, Bruce and Jamie Benidickson. *The Temagami Experience: Recreation, Resource and Aboriginal Rights in Northern Ontario Wilderness*. Toronto: University of Toronto Press, 1989.

Hodgins, Bruce and Margaret Hobbs. *Nastawagan: The Canadian North by Canoe & Snowshoe*. Toronto: Betelgeuse Books, 1985.

Ministry of Natural Resources, Blind River District. *Dunlop Lake – Flack Lake Canoe Route* pamphlet. 1984.

Ministry of Natural Resources, Chapleau District. *Chapleau–Nemegosenda River Provincial Park Canoe Route* map. 1984.

Ministry of Natural Resources, Chapleau District. *Wakami River Canoe Route* pamphlet. 1999.

Ministry of Natural Resources, Gogama Area Office, Timmins District. *4M Circle Canoe Route* pamphlet. Courtesy of Gogama Chamber of Commerce and Gogama Tourist and Outfitters. 1999.

Ministry of Natural Resources, Gogama Area Office, Timmins District. *Nabakawasi River Canoe Route* pamphlet. Courtesy of Gogama Chamber of Commerce and Gogama Tourist and Outfitters. 1999.

Ministry of Natural Resources, North Bay District. *Marten River Provincial Park Canoe Route* pamphlet.1984

Ministry of Natural Resources.*Ontario Living Legacy Land Use Strategy*, 1999.

Ministry of Natural Resources, Parks and Recreational Areas Branch, in cooperation with McClelland and Stewart. *Ontario Canoe Routes*. Toronto: 1981.

Ministry of Natural Resources. *Sudbury Area Canoe Route Map*. Toronto: 1977

Ministry of Natural Resources, Terrace Bay District. *Steel River Provincial Park Canoe Route* map. 1989

Ministry of Natural Resources, Thunder Bay District. *Wabakimi Provincial Park Information Package*. 1999

Ministry of Natural Resources, Timmins District. *Tatachikapika River Canoe Route* pamphlet. 1984.

Ministry of Natural Resources, Temagami District. *Canoeing in the Temagami Area* (map). Temagami, Ontario.

Preslie, Dave. "Personal Journal Entries on the Steel River." 2001.

Rand, Mac. *Paddles Flashing in the Sun: The Stories of Pathfinder in Algonquin Park*. West Seneca, NY: Centre Page 4 Inc. & Quaker Park Press, 1995.

Recommendations for the Algoma Headwaters Provincial Park Management Plan. Prepared by the Wildlands League and Friends of Algoma Highlands Park, 2000.

Reid, Ron and Janet Grand. *Canoeing Ontario's Rivers*. Vancouver/Toronto: Douglas & McIntyre, 1985.

Reid, Ron. "The Trappers of Wabakimi Lake." *Seasons*. Toronto: Federation of Ontario Naturalists, summer 1981.

Stimpson, Rob and Laurie. "Strange Happenings in the Boreal Forest." *Voyageur Magazine*. Ottawa: Nov./Dec. 1998.

Sundstedt, David. "Personal Journal Entries on the Steel River." 2000.

Taim, Astrid. *Almaguin: A Highland History*. Toronto: Natural Heritage/Natural History Inc., 1998.

Wilson, Hap. *Temagami Canoe Routes*. Toronto: Ontario Ministry of Natural Resources, 1977.

Zyvatkauskas, Betty. *Naturally Ontario: Exploring the Wealth of Ontario's Wild Places*. Toronto: Random House of Canada, 1999.

Web Resources
www.adventures.org
www.algonquincanada.com/way_of_tom_thomson1.htm
www.bonncherevalleytwp.com/ehistory.html
www.canadiancanoeroutes.com
www.chapleau.com/sultan/wakami.htm
www.home.golden.net/~bcaron/steellog2.htm
www.mcmichael.com
www.nob.on.ca/archives/apr95story/tourist.htm
www.noront.net/gonorth/adventures/canoeing.html
www.ontariolivinglegacy.com/algoma.html
www.ontarionature.org
www.ontariowilderness.com/images/lakes/gord_map_lake.jpg
www.ottertooth.com
wwwpastforward.ca/perspectives/July142000.htm
www.pcoutfitters.on.ca/nssteel%20river.htm
www.tbaytel.net/jhorn/areamap.htm
www.tomthomson.org
www.wabakimi.on.ca

explore

CANADA'S OUTDOOR ADVENTURE MAGAZINE

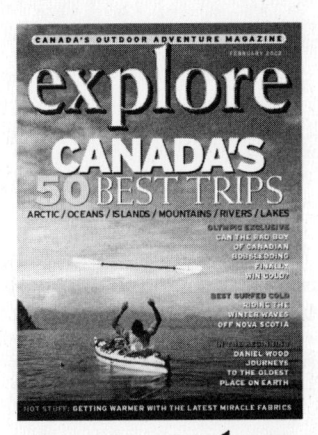

is proud to
have been a sponsor of
Kevin Callan's
expeditions to rediscover
Ontario's lost canoe routes.
And we hope that many, many
more canoeists will
follow in Kevin's wake.

HAPPY PADDLING!

Check us out at
www.explore-mag.com

MORE PADDLING BOOKS
FROM BOSTON MILLS PRESS

The BOSTON MILLS PRESS

A Conspiracy of Paddlers
31 Trips, 20 Trippers & Vital Tips for
Paddling Canada's Waterways
Edited by Alister Thomas
6 X 9 • SOFTCOVER • 304 PAGES • B&W PHOTOS
1-55046-390-X • $24.95 CDN • $19.95 US

Paddle Quest
Canada's Best Canoe Routes
Edited by Alister Thomas
6 X 9 • SOFTCOVER • 304 PAGES • B&W PHOTOS
1-55046-311-X • $24.95 CDN • $19.95 US

Stories from the Bow Seat
The Wisdom & Waggery of Canoe Tripping
Don Standfield and Liz Lundell
11.5 X 10 • HARDCOVER • 156 PAGES •
COLOR THROUGHOUT
1-55046-188-5 • $49.95 CDN • $37.95 US

Cradle to Canoe
Camping and Canoeing with Children
Rolf & Debra Kraiker
6 X 9 • SOFTCOVER • 168 PAGES • B&W WITH
8 PAGES COLOR
1-55046-294-6 • $19.95 CDN • $18.95 US

Cottage Country Canoe Routes
Kevin Callan
7 X 9 • SOFTCOVER • 96 PAGES • MAPS •
60 COLOR PHOTOS
1-55046-071-4 • $19.95 CDN • $15.95 US

Killarney
Kevin Callan
10 X 10 • SOFTCOVER • 80 PAGES • COLOR THROUGHOUT
1-55046-0188 • $16.95 CDN • $13.50 US

The Soft Paddling Guide
to Ontario and New England
Jonathon Reynolds & Heather Smith
6 X 9 • SOFTCOVER • 168 PAGES • MAPS •
COLOR THROUGHOUT
1-55046-335-7 • $29.95 CDN • $16.95 US

Kayaking Georgian Bay
Jonathon Reynolds & Heather Smith
6 X 9 • SOFTCOVER • 168 PAGES • B&W WITH MAPS
1-55046-280-6 • $19.95 CDN • $13.95 US

Northern Saskatchewan Canoe Trips
A Guide to 15 Wilderness Rivers
Laurel Archer
6 X 9 • SOFTCOVER • 240 PAGES • MAPS •
8-PAGE COLOR INSERT
1-55046-369-1 • $24.95 CDN • $19.95 US

Wilderness Manitoba
Land Where the Spirit Lives
Hap Wilson & Stephanie Aykroyd
11 X 8.5 • HARDCOVER • 144 PAGES •
100 COLOR PHOTOS
1-55046-271-7 • $24.95 CDN • $19.95 US

Where Rivers Run
Gary & Joanie McGuffin
5.5 X 8.75 • SOFTCOVER • 242 PAGES • MAPS •
ILLUSTRATIONS • 8 PAGES COLOR
1-55046-314-4 • $22.95 CDN • $18.95 US

Superior
Journeys on an Inland Sea
Gary & Joanie McGuffin
11.5 X 10 • HARDCOVER • 160 PAGES •
COLOR THROUGHOUT
1-55046-067-6 • $50 CDN • $40 US

Paddle Your Own Canoe
Gary & Joanie McGuffin
11 X 8.5 • 208 PAGES • OVER 600 COLOR
PHOTOS & ILLUSTRATIONS
1-55046-214-8 • HARDCOVER • $39.95 CDN • $29.95 US
1-55046-377-2 • SOFTCOVER • $29.95 CDN • $19.95 US

Dangerous River
Adventure on the Nahanni
R.M. Patterson
5.5 X 8.75 • SOFTCOVER • 276 PAGES
1-55046-316-0 • $22.95 CDN • $18.95 US

Canoescapes
Bill Mason
11.5 X 10 • HARDCOVER • 160 PAGES •
COLOR THROUGHOUT
1-55046-141-9 • $50 CDN • $40 US

French River
Canoeing the River of the Stick-Wavers
Toni Harting
9 X 9 • SOFTCOVER • 160 PAGES • COLOR INSERT
1-55046-163-X • $22.95 CDN • $18.95 US

For additional Boston Mills Press titles, visit our website at www.bostonmillspress.com